HOT TOPICS

Hands-on activities ● Investigations ● Model-making ... and much more!

Castles

ages 5-11
for all primary years

Peter Riley

Author
Peter Riley

Editor
Catherine Gilhooly

Assistant Editor
Niamh O'Carroll

Cover and inside illustrations
Laszlo Veres/Beehive Illustration

Photocopiable page illustrations
Colin Elgie

Back cover and inside photography
Peter Rowe

Model-making
Linda Jones

Polaroid photos
Linda Jones. Except pages 19 (bottom), 26, 29, 43 and 59, Peter Rowe.

Series Designer
Helen Taylor

Designer
Andrea Lewis

Cover concept/designer
Helen Taylor

Text © 2007 Peter Riley

© 2007 Scholastic Ltd

Designed using Adobe InDesign

Published by Scholastic Ltd
Book End
Range Road
Witney
Oxfordshire OX29 0YD

www.scholastic.co.uk

Printed in China through Golden Cup Printing Services
3 4 5 6 7 8 9   0 1 2 3 4 5 6

British Library Cataloguing-in-Publication Data
A catalogue record for this book is available from the British Library.

ISBN 978-0439-94510-3

The rights of the author Peter Riley have been asserted in accordance with the Copyright, Designs and Patents Act 1988.

Crown copyright material is reproduced under the terms of the Click Use Licence.

The publishers gratefully acknowledge:
Early Learning Centre for the use of knights and jousting figures for photography www.elc.co.uk
Warwick Castle for the use of their photographs www.warwick-castle.co.uk

Contents

IMAGE © COREL

Introduction

The *Hot Topics* series explores topics that can be taught across the curriculum. Each book divides its topic into a number of themes that can be worked through progressively to build up a firm foundation of knowledge and provide opportunities for developing a wide range of skills. Each theme provides background information and three lesson plans for ages 5–7, 7–9 and 9–11. Each lesson plan looks at a different aspect of the theme and varies in complexity from a simple approach with younger children to a more complex approach with older children. There are also one or more photocopiable pages to support the lessons in each theme.

BACKGROUND INFORMATION
Each theme starts by providing information to support you in teaching the lesson. You may share it with the children as part of your own lesson plan or use it to help answer some of the children's questions as they arise. Information is also given about the material on the photocopiable sheets as well as the answers to any questions that have been set. This section also provides a brief overview of all three lessons to help you select the content for your own lessons.

The lessons
A detailed structure is provided for lessons aimed at children who are in the 7–9 age range. Less detailed lesson plans, covering all the essentials, are given for the lessons aimed at the other two age ranges, so covering the entire primary age range.

Detailed lesson plans
The detailed lesson plans have the following format:

Objectives
These are general objectives related to the study of castles.

Subject references
All lesson plans show how they relate to specific curriculum-related objectives. These objectives are based on statements in the National Curriculum in England. They may be used as they are or regarded as an illustration of the statements that may be addressed, helping you to find others which you consider more appropriate for your needs.

Resources and preparation
This section provides a list of everything you will need to deliver the lesson including any photocopiables provided in this book. Preparation describes anything that needs to be done in advance of the lesson such as purchasing a toy bow and arrow, preparing word cards, and so on. As part of the preparation you should consult your school's policies on all practical work so that you can select activities for which you are confident to take responsibility. The ASE publication *Be Safe!* (ISBN 0-863-57324-X) gives useful guidance for conducting safe science activities.

Starter

A Starter is only provided in the more detailed lesson plans for ages 7–9. It provides an introduction to the lesson and helps the children to focus on the topic and generate interest.

What to do

This section sets out, point by point, the sequence of activities in the main part of the lesson. It may include activities for you to do but mainly concentrates on the children's work.

Differentiation

This section is only provided in lesson plans for ages 7–9. Suggestions are given for developing strategies for support and extension activities.

Assessment

This section is only provided in lesson plans for the 7-9 age range. It suggests ways to assess children either through the product of their work or through looking at how they performed in an activity.

Plenary

A Plenary is only provided in lesson plans for ages 7–9. It shows how children can review their own work and assess their progress in learning about castles. It is not related to other lessons but if you are planning a sequence of lessons you may also like to use it to generate interest in future castle studies.

Outcomes

These are only provided in the lesson plans for the 7-9 age range. They relate to the general objectives. You may wish to add more specific outcomes related to the context in which you used the lesson.

Extension

This section is found in the lesson plans for 5–7 and 9–11 year olds. It allows you to take the initial content of the lesson further.

Flexibility and extra differentiation

As the lessons in each topic are clustered around a particular theme you may wish to add parts of one lesson to parts of another. For example, in Theme 2 'The gatehouse', you may wish to add the assembly of the portcullis in Lesson 2 to Lesson 1, so it becomes 'The gatehouse and portcullis'.

In the lesson plans for 7–9 year olds, differentiation is addressed directly with its own section. In lessons for the other age groups differentiation is addressed by providing ideas for extension work. However, the themes are arranged so that you may also pick activities from the different age groups to provide differentiation. For example, in a lesson for ages 5–7, you may wish to add activities from the lesson for 7–9 year olds in the same theme.

Planning a project

You may like to use the topic for a class or whole-school project culminating in a Castle Day. This of course will need considerable preparation but the result could be a very memorable event. This section provides some suggestions for activities leading up to the day and a programme of events.

The activities in the tables in this section are based on activities in the lesson plans shown in the third column. Read through each lesson plan and work out how you will use or develop the activity in the context of your Castle Day.

Times are given in the first column for guidance only. Depending on your circumstances you may wish to lengthen or shorten any of the activities.

Castle Day: ages 5–7
Preparation

- If appropriate, send a letter home asking for parents to help make medieval costumes. Ideas for costumes can be found at **www.medieval-banquet.co.uk**. If you feel that some children will not be able to bring a costume, gather together some items that they could use.
- In the letter, mention that a feature of the day will be a feast, and check with parents and carers for children's food allergies or dietary requirements. Provide them with a list of suitable medieval foods for children to bring in (Theme 6 Lesson 3).
- Rehearse the following herald to say at the procession:

    Hail good people of this place,
    Prepare for fun, make haste, make haste,
    'Tis time to work , 'tis time to play,
    On this our special Castle Day!

You could replace the word 'special' with the name of the school, class or year group taking part.

- Provide a CD of medieval music or perform the music for the castle dance at the procession (Theme 6 Lesson 2).

Ages 5–7		Activity	Lesson plan	Pages
MORNING	10 minutes	Take part in a costume procession	Castle people Theme 4 Lesson 1	34
	40 minutes	Make a model stone castle	A kingdom of castles Theme 1 Lesson 2	10/14
	30 minutes	Explore how a bow and arrow works	Archery Theme 7 Lesson 1	58/62
	40 minutes	Make a shield to put on the wall	Heraldry Theme 5 Lesson 1	42/46
	10 minutes	Find out how people ate in medieval times	Preparing a feast Theme 6 lesson 3	53
AFTERNOON	15 minutes	Watch a play about a boy who becomes a knight	The making of a knight Theme 5 lesson 3	45/48
	40 minutes	Hold a mini jousting competition	Jousting Theme 6 Lesson 1	50/54
	30 minutes	Compare the effects of medieval weapons by knocking down castle walls	Trebuchet and cannon Theme 8 Lesson 1	66/70
	15 minutes	Listen to a medieval story in a pretend castle setting	Bodwin's bouncy castle Theme 9 lesson 1	74/78

HOTTOPICS Castles

Castle Day: ages 7–9
Preparation

- If appropriate, send a letter home asking for parents to help make medieval costumes. Try **www.medieval-banquet.co.uk** for ideas. If some children are unlikely to be able to bring a costume, collect some items they could use.
- Check for food allergies or dietary requirements, and provide a list of medieval foods for children to bring in (Theme 6 Lesson 3).
- Rehearse the following herald to say at the procession:

    Hail good people of this place,
    Prepare for fun, make haste, make haste,
    'Tis time to work, 'tis time to play,
    On this our special Castle Day!

You could replace the word 'special' with the name of the school, class or year group taking part.
- Provide a CD of medieval music or perform the music for the castle dance at the procession (Theme 6 Lesson 2).
- Rehearse the castle dance (Theme 6 Lesson 2).

Castle Day: ages 9–11
Preparation

- If appropriate, send a letter home asking for parents to help make medieval costumes. For children who are unlikely to be able to bring a costume, gather together some items they could use.
- Check for children's food allergies or dietary requirements, and provide a list of medieval foods for children to bring in for the feast. (Theme 6 Lesson 3).
- Plan together how to turn the classroom into a Great Hall, leaving spaces on the walls for individual coats of arms (Theme 6 Lesson 3).
- The idea behind the day is to hold a feast to celebrate two squires becoming knights. Some children will need to learn the accompanying music beforehand (Theme 6 Lesson 2).
- Rehearse the castle dance (Theme 6 Lesson 2).

Ages 7–9		Activity	Lesson plan	Pages
MORNING	10 minutes	Take part in a procession of costumes	Castle people Theme 4 Lesson 1	34
	30 minutes	Explore how a bow and arrow works	Archery Theme 7 Lesson 1	58/62
	30 minutes	Find out how to make and use a trebuchet	The trebuchet Theme 7 Lesson 2	59/63
	40 minutes	Make a shield to put on the wall	Heraldry Theme 5 Lesson 1	42/46
	40 minutes	Find out how people ate in medieval times	Preparing a feast Theme 6 lesson 3	53
AFTERNOON	15 minutes	Watch a play about a boy who becomes a knight	The making of a knight Theme 5 lesson 3	45/48
	40 minutes	Hold a competition on making suits of armour	Armour Theme 5 Lesson 2	43/47
	40 minutes	Listen to stories about haunted castles	The haunted castle Theme 9 lesson 2	75/79
	30 minutes	Final rehearsal and performance of the castle dance	Music and dance Theme 6 lesson 2	51/55/56

Ages 9–11		Activity	Lesson plan	Pages
MORNING	30 minutes	Explore the making of a knight (this could be used as a dress rehearsal for the performance later)	The making of a knight Theme 5 lesson 3	45/48
	40 minutes	Make your own shield and hang it in the Great Hall	Heraldry Theme 5 Lesson 1	42/46
	40 minutes	Listen to stories about haunted castles	The haunted castle Theme 9 Lesson 2	75/79
	10 minutes	Find out how people ate in medieval times	Preparing a feast Theme 6 lesson 3	53
AFTERNOON	15 minutes	Performance of 'The making of a knight' play	The making of a knight Theme 5 lesson 3	45/48
	15 minutes	Perform the castle dance	Music and dance Theme 6 lesson 2	51/55/56
	40 minutes	Play the board game 'Siege'.	Siege Theme 7 lesson 3	61/64
	30 minutes	Look at castles across the country	Finding out about castles Theme 1 lesson 3	12/15/16
	15 minutes	Convert the Great Hall back into a classroom		

Introducing castles

BACKGROUND

Castles provided a well defended home for a powerful family. They were built to protect people from the quick and deadly attack of cavalry. A castle was always built around a well. This provided water for the people to drink if the castle was held under siege.

An early form of castle was the 'motte and bailey' castle. The 'motte' was an earth mound on which a tower was constructed and the 'bailey' was a courtyard in which people and animals could shelter. A flying bridge connected the bailey to the top of the motte. People would run up here if they thought the bailey defences would not hold.

Later castles were built of stone and had a large central tower called the 'keep' surrounded by walls called 'curtain walls'. There was a gatehouse on one wall to allow people to enter and leave.

THE CONTENTS
Lesson 1 (Ages 5–7)
Making a motte and bailey castle
The children look at the picture of the motte and bailey castle, then cut out and paste the components.

Lesson 2 (Ages 7–9)
A kingdom of castles
The children begin by considering the feudal system and how land was divided up. They cut out simple castles and set them up in a classroom 'kingdom'.

Lesson 3 (Ages 9–11)
Finding out about castles
The children use a map to identify three of the nearest castles to where they live. They use the internet to visit the castles and to make a report.

Notes on photocopiables
Motte and bailey castle (page 13)
This sheet provides templates to create a motte and bailey castle. Figure A is the palisade around the bailey, B is the palisade at the top of the motte, C1 and C2 are palisades on either side of D, the flying bridge. Figure E is a tower.

A castle of stone (page 14)
Some children may need help with cutting out and assembling objects. Make sure they do not cut off the tabs.

Castles and their locations (page 15)
A number of castles are named and brief information is given to locate their positions using a map of The British Isles.

Castles map (page 16)
This map features the locations of a number of castles around The British Isles, labelled A–U. The answers are:
A) Doe; B) Donegal; C) Dundrum;
D) Dunluce; E) Duntreath; F) Dunrobin;
G) Drum; H) Airlee; I) Aberdour;
J) Bamburgh; K) Richmond;
L) Knaresborough; M) Skipton;
N) Tamworth; O) Warwick; P) Hever;
Q) Corfe; R) Caerphilly; S) Pembroke;
T) Caernarvon; U) Ewloe.

PHOTOGRAPH © PHOTODISC/GETTY IMAGES

Lesson 1 Making a motte and bailey castle

Resources and preparation
● Photocopy the castle template from page 13, 'Motte and bailey castle', onto paper or card, for each group.
● Assemble a castle beforehand and set it up in a sand tray. The motte should be approximately 14cm across and its top should be about 5cm high.
● Place the castle as shown in the diagram on the photocopiable sheet and scrape a ditch around it. This should help you judge how much sand is needed for each tray.
● Provide a sand tray, scissors and glue for each group.
● For the Extension, you will need a large outdoor area, such as the school field.

What to do
● Show the children the picture of the motte and bailey castle on page 13. Tell them the names of the different parts and ask them to complete the stakes on the palisades (figures A, B, C1 and C2) and the steps on the flying bridge (figure D), by drawing vertical lines along them. Note the positions of the tabs on the two long palisades (figures A and B), and on the shorter palisades (figures C1 and C2).
● Ask the children to cut out the items. Assemble the motte and bailey palisades by making them into circles and gluing the ends together at the tabs.
● Fold down the supports on each side of the flying bridge and fold down the tabs of the palisades that will flank it. (**Tip**: It works better if C1 and C2 are folded in opposite directions.)
● Let the children assemble the tower and make it secure by gluing the tabs.
● Challenge each group to make a motte out of sand and place the tower and palisade around it.
● Position the bailey palisade at one side of the motte. Connect the two by leaning the flying bridge up the motte so that the doors are lined up. Then attach the palisades to protect the bridge.
● Tell the children to dig out a ditch around the castle except in front of the door. Explain that in a real castle there would be a drawbridge and you are going to make one in the next lesson.

Extension
Explain that the base of a motte would have been about 60 metres in diameter and measure this out on the school field. The top of a motte would have been 36 metres across. Measure this out inside the area you have previously marked.

AGES 5–7

Objectives
● To understand the structure of the first castles.
● To make a simple model.
● To use a range of materials, including sand, safely.

Subject references
History
● Use common words and phrases relating to the passing of time.
(NC: KS1 1b)
● Recognise why people did things.
(NC: KS1 2a)
● The way of life of people in the more distant past who lived in the local area or elsewhere in Britain.
(NC: KS1 6b)
Design and technology
● Assemble, join and combine materials and components.
(NC: KS1 2d)
Mathematics
● Compare and measure objects using uniform non-standard units, then with a standard unit of length.
(NC: KS1 Ma3 4a)

PHOTOGRAPH © PETER ROWE

Lesson 2 A kingdom of castles

AGES 7–9

Objectives
- To understand that castles were built to defend areas of land.
- To understand how the land in a kingdom was divided up.
- To give children an opportunity to work together as group.

Subject references
History
- Place people and changes into correct periods of time. (NC: KS2 1a)
- Understand the characteristic features of the periods studied. (NC: KS2 2a)
- Understand the social diversity of the society studied. (NC: KS2 2b)

Art and design
- Explore ideas for different purposes. (NC: KS2 1a)
- Use a variety of approaches to communicate ideas. (NC: KS2 2c)

Resources and preparation
- Photocopy page 14, 'A castle of stone', onto paper or card, for each group. (You may wish to enlarge it in size.)
- Assemble a castle beforehand so that you can anticipate any problems that the children might have when making their models.
- You will need scissors, glue, coloured pencils and scrap paper for each group.
- This lesson can be adapted to be part of your Castle Day.

Starter
- Invite the children to imagine that they are a king, whose army has just invaded a country. It is too big for a king to ride around all the time and defend it. Ask how the children would set about defending it.
- After listening to suggestions, steer the discussion towards the king selecting a few of the soldiers in his army to defend certain areas of it. Explain that each of these soldiers could be made a lord and allocated a group of other soldiers to help him defend his area of land. The lords could then build castles in which to live with their men and their families. To identify their castles, the lords created a banner of their own design which is flown from their castle.
- Tell the children that you are the king who has just invaded a country (represented by the classroom) and in order to defend it, you are appointing a lord on each table to organise the building of a castle. (The lord does not always have to be a boy).

What to do
- Appoint a lord to each table and give them a copy of the photocopiable sheet. The lord must organise the other children on the table to cut out and assemble the castle. While this is being done, the lord can work on scrap paper to make a design for the banner.
- When the castle is ready, the lord must instruct the other children in their group to put the design on both sides of the banners that are provided on the photocopiable sheet. The largest banner should be flown from the tower and the others from each tower on either side of the castle.

Differentiation
- Some children may need the assistance of an adult helper in cutting out and assembling the castle.
- Invite more confident learners to look at pictures of real castles in books or on the internet and to draw in windows and arrow loops on their castles before they assemble them. They could also look at the types of banner designs and motifs that were used in the medieval period to inspire them when creating their own flags.

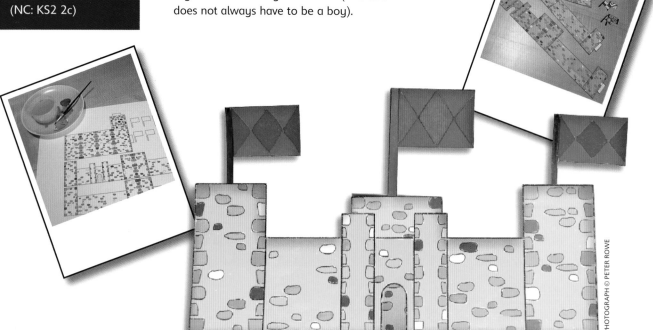

PHOTOGRAPH © PETER ROWE

ILLUSTRATION © LASZLO VERES/BEEHIVE ILLUSTRATION

Assessment

Assess the children on how well they work together and follow instructions from each other. Look at the quality of the banner design, for example, are they simple and clear, or is there too much detail included in the design? Have children been creative and original or perhaps successfully used research to influence their decorations and designs? Assess the cutting out and pasting together of the components.

Plenary

Set the scene by telling the children that as king you will travel around your kingdom and visit each castle in turn. Explain that you will be judging each castle's suitability for defending part of your kingdom. Ask the class to decide on an appropriate 'punishment' to give to a lord who has not produced a satisfactory castle. Let them know however, that as king, you have the right to pardon a lord whose castle needs further attention.

Outcomes

- The children understand how castles were set up to defend a kingdom.
- The children work together successfully on a task.

Did you know?

A knight could ride about 16 kilometres in any direction around a castle to defend its lands.

Lesson 3 Finding out about castles

AGES 9–11

Objectives
● To locate castles on a map.
● To find out which castle is nearest to the school.
● To use the internet to find out about castles

Subject references
Geography
● Identify and describe where places are.
(NC: KS2 3b)
ICT
● Talk about what information they need and how they can find and use it
(NC: KS2 1a)
● To develop then end with NC: KS2 2a.
● To develop and refine ideas by organising text and images.
(NC: KS2 2a)

Resources and preparation
● Make copies photocopiable page 15, 'Castles and their locations', and photocopiable page 16 'Castles map'.
● Provide a map of the United Kingdom and Republic of Ireland showing all the major towns.
● This lesson can be adapted to be part of your Castle Day.

What to do
● Show the children a map of the United Kingdom and make sure that they can identify north, south, east and west.
● Work with the class to locate the region where they live on the map.
● Give each child a copy of 'Castles and their locations' and 'Castles map' photocopiable sheets. Explain that 'The castles map' shows the position of 21 castles around The United Kingdom and Republic of Ireland. Lead the children in skimming the other photocopiable sheet to ascertain that it lists the names of the castles and information on how to find them using a map.
● Let the children use the maps available and the information on the 'Castles and their locations' page to locate the castles and label them on their copy of 'Castles map'.

● Encourage the children to work out which is the nearest castle to their school and which is the farthest away.
● Challenge the children to calculate the distances between their school and the nearest and furthest castles, in kilometres and in miles.

Extension
● The websites **www.castleuk.net** and **www.castlexplorer.co.uk/maps.php** provide photographs, pictures and straightforward information about many castles. The children could use the internet to find a number of castles in the region around where they live and write a report on what they discover.
● Encourage more confident learners to prepare their report using ICT, selecting different font sizes and styles, including images and adding hyperlinks.

PHOTOGRAPH © TIM LARGE, STOCK.XCHNG

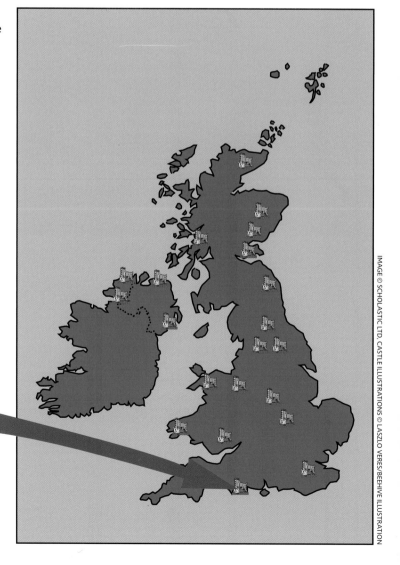

IMAGE © SCHOLASTIC LTD. CASTLE ILLUSTRATIONS © LASZLO VERES/BEEHIVE ILLUSTRATION

Theme 1 Motte and bailey castle

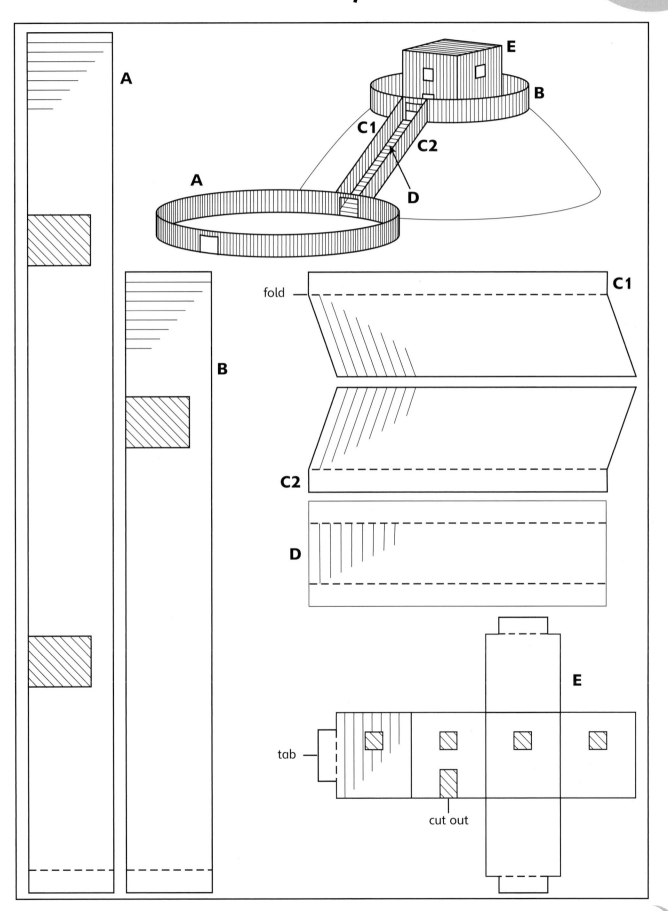

■SCHOLASTIC
www.scholastic.co.uk

Theme 1 A castle of stone

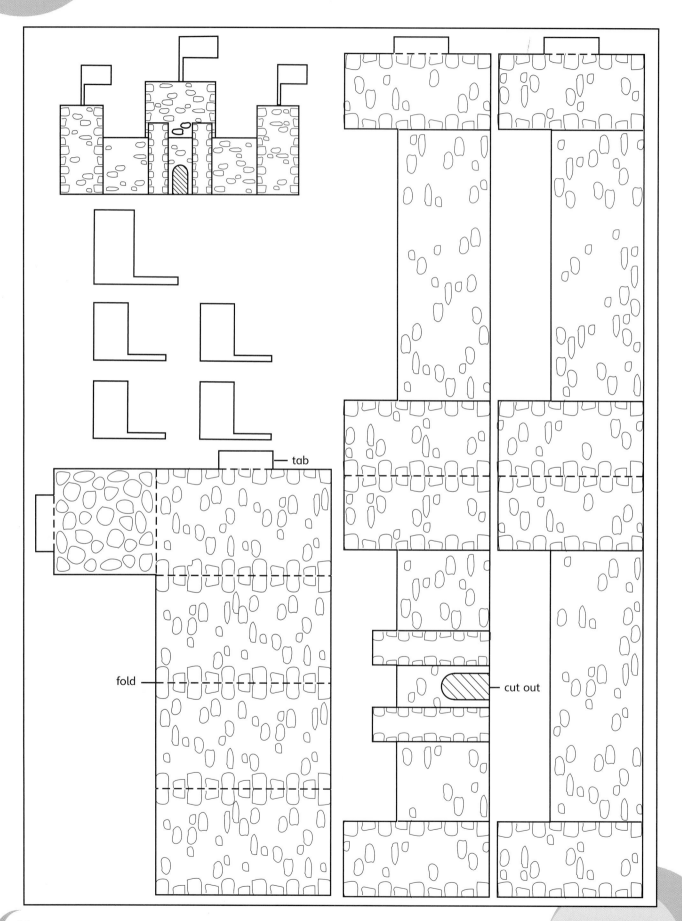

tab

fold

cut out

Theme 1 Castles and their locations

Northern Ireland and Ireland	
Castle	**Location**
Doe	West of Londonderry
Donegal	West of Omagh
Dundrum	South of Belfast
Dunluce	North of Coleraine

Scotland	
Castle	**Location**
Aberdour	North of Edinburgh
Airlee	North of Dundee
Drum	West of Aberdeen
Dunrobin	South-west of Wick
Duntreath	North of Glasgow

England	
Castle	**Location**
Richmond	South-west of Darlington
Knaresborough	North of Harrogate
Skipton	North-west of Leeds
Bamburgh	South of Berwick on Tweed
Tamworth	North of Birmingham
Warwick	South of Coventry
Hever	South of London
Corfe	West of Bournemouth

Wales	
Castle	**Location**
Caerphilly	North of Cardiff
Pembroke	West of Tenby
Caernarvon	South of the Isle of Anglesey
Ewloe	West of Chester

Theme 1 Castles map

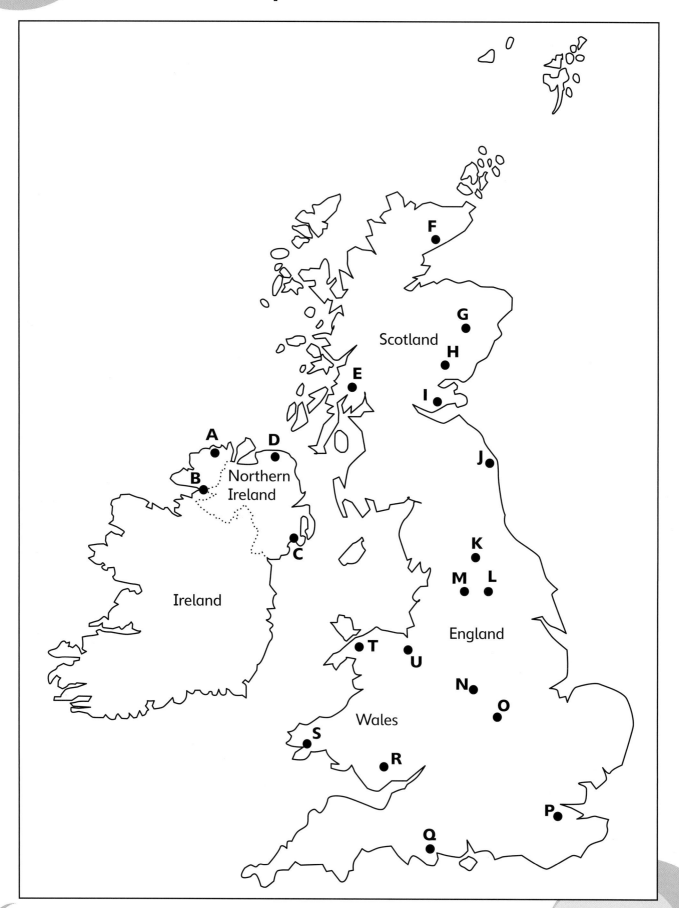

The gatehouse

BACKGROUND

The weakest point of a castle was the entrance. Compared to the thick stone walls, the gate was made of a thinner layer of weaker material – wood. It could be smashed open with a battering ram if there was nothing there to protect it. Many castles were surrounded by a moat. This prevented the enemy tunnelling up to the walls (see Theme 3). The drawbridge could be lifted when the castle was under attack.

Behind the drawbridge, the portcullis could be lowered to provide further protection. The points on its lower edge could impale attackers. The portcullis moved in grooves down the walls, which prevented it from being forced back like a door. The drawbridge and portcullis were raised and lowered using winches, but these have been omitted from the lesson models for simplicity.

The gatehouse had rooms above the entrance that housed the winches. It may also have had a room with holes in the floor called 'murder holes'. If the enemy got close to the gates, hot sand, boiling water or stones could be dropped onto them through the holes. Some gatehouses had an area in front or behind the gates called the barbican. If the enemy reached these areas they could be fired at from front battlements close by.

The gatehouse was the home of the constable, who ran the castle when the lord was absent. Gates were permanently guarded by sentries, who would check people entering the castle. There were rooms in which the sentries could rest. At night the gates were closed and a heavy wooden bar was placed across them on the inside. Some gatehouses displayed the castle lord's coat of arms.

THE CONTENTS
Lesson 1 (Ages 5–7)
The gatehouse and drawbridge
The children build a gatehouse with a drawbridge that they can raise and lower.

Lesson 2 (Ages 7–9)
The drawbridge and portcullis
The children build a gatehouse with a drawbridge and portcullis that they can raise and lower.

Lesson 3 (Ages 9–11)
The gatehouse defences
The children build a gatehouse with a drawbridge, portcullis, doors and passageway with murder holes.

Notes on photocopiables
Gatehouse and drawbridge (page 22)
Figure 1 shows the gatehouse from the back, indicating how the front is turned back at lines AB and CD, and how the support is fastened across the bottom. The drawbridge is attached with a piece of sticky tape at point X and two pieces of string at Y.

Portcullis (page 23)
Figure 1 shows the gatehouse from Lesson 1 from the back, showing one of the lugs in place to which the cylindrical bar is attached to pull the portcullis string over. It also shows how the grooves A and B are folded and fit on either side of the door.

Doors and murder holes (page 24)
This sheet has passageway and door templates. Figure 1 shows the back of the gatehouse with the passageway, doors and murder holes in position.

PHOTOGRAPH © JERRY PANK, STOCK.XCHANGE

Lesson 1 The gatehouse and drawbridge

Resources and preparation
● Photocopy the template from page 22, 'Gatehouse and drawbridge', onto paper or card, for each group.
● You will need scissors, glue, sticky tape, and two pieces of very thin string or thread 30cm long.
● Assemble a gatehouse beforehand so that you can anticipate any problems that the children might have.

What to do
● You may like to do this as a demonstration with the children helping you or let older children work together on this activity.
● Give out the photocopiable sheet and tell the children to cut out the gatehouse. Cut out the holes for the string for them when they are ready and make a hole so that the children can cut out the doorway.
● Ask the children to cut out the base support and show them how to fasten it in place.

● Direct the children to attach the drawbridge loosely to point X using sticky tape.
● Explain that they need to attach one end of each string to the drawbridge at the points marked Y and then thread the string through the holes in the gatehouse. Encourage the children to experiment with different materials for this: they could try selecting glue or sticky tape.
● Finally, challenge the children to stand up their gatehouse model and demonstrate how they can raise and lower the drawbridge.

Extension
Show the children pictures of a gatehouse and ask them to imagine that they are coming up to the castle. What do they think about the castle? What do they think might be inside? Ask them to imagine that they are being chased by an enemy. How would they feel if they saw the gatehouse now? Let the children discuss their ideas, then write about them or draw a picture.

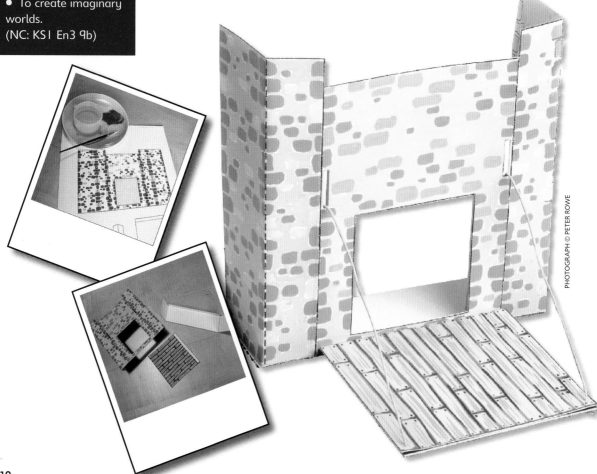

PHOTOGRAPH © PETER ROWE

Lesson 2 The drawbridge and portcullis

Resources and preparation
- Photocopy the templates from page 22, 'Gatehouse and drawbridge', and page 23, 'Portcullis', onto card or paper.
- You will need scissors, glue, sticky tape, two pieces of very thin string or thread, 30cm long for the drawbridge, plus a piece of string about 25cm long to attach to the portcullis.
- Assemble a gatehouse beforehand so that you can anticipate any problems that the children might have.

Starter
- Tell the children that many castles had a moat around them and ask for a reason. Look for an answer about stopping the enemy reaching the castle walls. Explain that in order for people to enter and leave the castle, the gatehouse also had to have a drawbridge.
- Ask the children if they know what a portcullis is. Ascertain that it was a type of gate, which dropped down and had spikes on it. Be prepared for tales of people meeting a gruesome end when hit by a portcullis! Explain that a gatehouse with a drawbridge and a portcullis was complicated to build.
- Challenge the children to try to make their own versions and to investigate the problems that castle builders had to deal with to make sure their gatehouse was secure.

What to do
- Give the children a copy of the 'Gatehouse and drawbridge' photocopiable sheet and let them cut out the gatehouse, rope holes and door way. Ask them to cut out the base support and fasten it to the back as Figure 1 shows.
- Next, invite the children to cut out the drawbridge and loosely attach it to point X with sticky tape. The drawbridge should move freely up and down.
- Instruct the children to attach one end of each piece of 30cm long string to the drawbridge, at the points marked Y, and to thread the string through the holes in the gatehouse. Encourage them to experiment with different materials for securing the string: they could try selecting glue or sticky tape and see which works better.
- Encourage the children to stand up their gatehouse model and demonstrate raising and lowering the drawbridge.
- Give out a copy of the 'Portcullis' photocopiable sheet and ask the children to cut out the grooves A and B. Help them to glue the grooves in place on either side of the doorway, using Figure 1 as a visual guide.
- Tell the children to cut out the lugs L and 'M, and stick them in place at the top of the battlement as the diagram shows.

AGES 7–9

Objectives
- To assemble the front of a gatehouse.
- To attach a drawbridge and raise and lower it on strings.
- To assemble a portcullis and lifting mechanism and make the portcullis go up and down.

Subject references
Design and technology
- Cut out and shape a range of materials, and assemble, join and combine components and materials accurately.
(NC: KS2 2d)
- Understand how mechanisms can be used to make things move in different ways.
(NC: KS2 4c)
Science
- Understand that objects are pulled downwards because of the gravitational attraction between them and the Earth.
(NC: KS2 Sc4 2b)
English
- Imagine and explore feelings and ideas, focusing on creative uses of language to interest the reader.
(NC: KS2 En3 9a)

PHOTOGRAPH © PETER ROWE

ILLUSTRATION © LASZLO VERES/BEEHIVE ILLUSTRATION

Did you know?

A gatehouse was the castle's control centre – like the bridge on a ship.

• Next, ask the children to cut out the cylindrical bar C, roll it up into a cylinder and make it secure by gluing and sticking its long tab. The cylinder can then be placed with the lugs going inside them as the picture shows.

• Invite the children to cut out the portcullis P, and attach one end of the 25cm long piece of string to point X with glue or sticky paper.

• Challenge the children to slide the portcullis into the grooves and run the string over the cylinder. Can they use the string to raise their portcullis?

Differentiation

• Some children may need help in cutting out rope holes and the doorway. They may be able to cut out the drawbridge and portcullis, and attach string to them, but require help with placing the grooves, lugs and cylinder.

• Encourage more confident learners to make a portcullis out of lollipop sticks or long, spent matches.

Assessment

The children can be assessed on the way they tackle some of the more intricate work when making the model. The models themselves can be assessed for ease of use and their state after being used at least ten times.

Plenary

Ask the children to imagine that they live in a castle and are walking back to it, when the watchman sounds a horn that means an enemy is approaching. The chains holding the drawbridge clank as it starts to move slowly upwards. In the gatehouse there is a rumble as the portcullis starts to come down. The children run and jump for the drawbridge. Ask them to write down what happens next. Give them a few minutes then invite them to read out their stories.

Outcomes

• The children can assemble a model gatehouse with a working drawbridge and portcullis.

Lesson 3 The gatehouse defences

Resources and preparation
● Photocopy the templates from 'Gatehouse and drawbridge', 'Portcullis' and 'Doors and murder holes' on photocopiable pages 22, 23 and 24 onto card or paper.
● Provide scissors, glue, sticky tape, two pieces of very thin string or thread, 30cm long for the drawbridge, plus a piece of string about 25cm long to attach to the portcullis.
● Assemble a gatehouse beforehand so that you can anticipate any problems that the children might have.

What to do
● Using the What to do sections in the previous lesson plans, build the gatehouse with the drawbridge and portcullis.
● Give the children a copy of the 'Doors and murder holes' sheet and ask them to cut out the doors, passageway and murder holes.
● They need to glue each door onto both

ends of the passageway so that they can be opened or closed. Then the children should glue and stick the tab along the base part of the passageway to close it up.
● Finally, tell the children to set up the doors and passageway with the gatehouse as shown in Figure 1.

Extension
Ask the children to imagine that they are at the front of an attacking army. The castle drawbridge has not been raised in time and they are being pushed across it by the soldiers behind them. The portcullis starts to come down and they and a few others are pushed under it before it falls. They can see their soldiers bringing a battering ram along the drawbridge but they are suddenly attacked by archers from the battlements. What should the children do? Give them a few minutes to write their stories then invite them to read them out.

Objectives
● To assemble the front of a gatehouse.
● To attach a drawbridge and raise and lower it on strings.
● To assemble a portcullis and lifting mechanism and make the portcullis go up and down.
● To assemble a passageway with murder holes and doors and place it behind the portcullis.

Subject references
Design and technology
● Cut and shape a range of materials, and assemble, join and combine components and materials accurately. (NC: KS2 2d)
● Understand how mechanisms can be used to make things move in different ways. (NC: KS2 4c)
English
● Imagine and explore feelings and ideas, focusing on creative uses of language to interest the reader. (NC: KS2 En3 9a)

PHOTOGRAPH © PETER ROWE, MODEL KNIGHTS © EARLY LEARNING CENTRE

Theme 2 Gatehouse and drawbridge

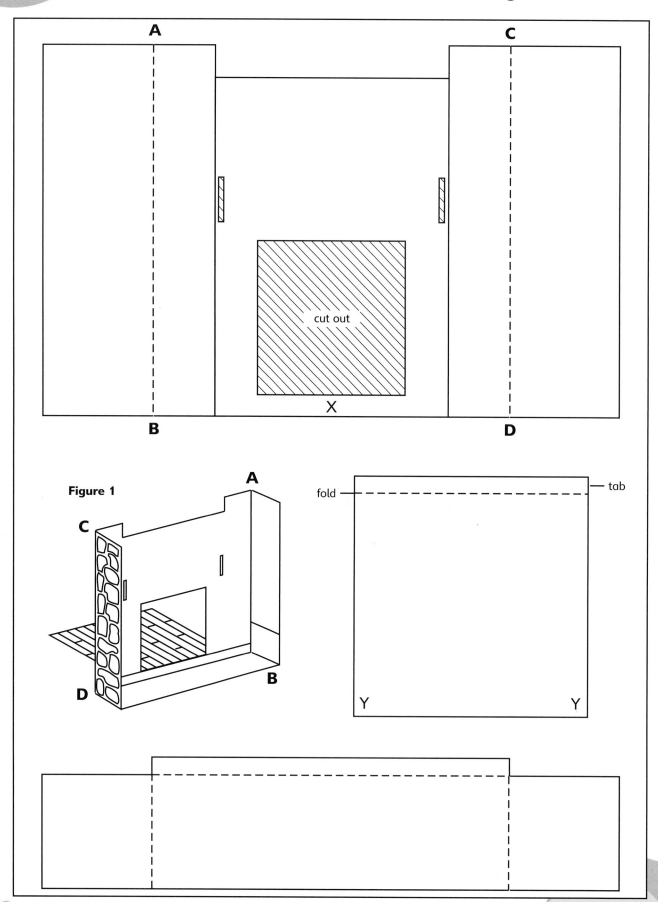

Figure 1

Theme 2 Portcullis

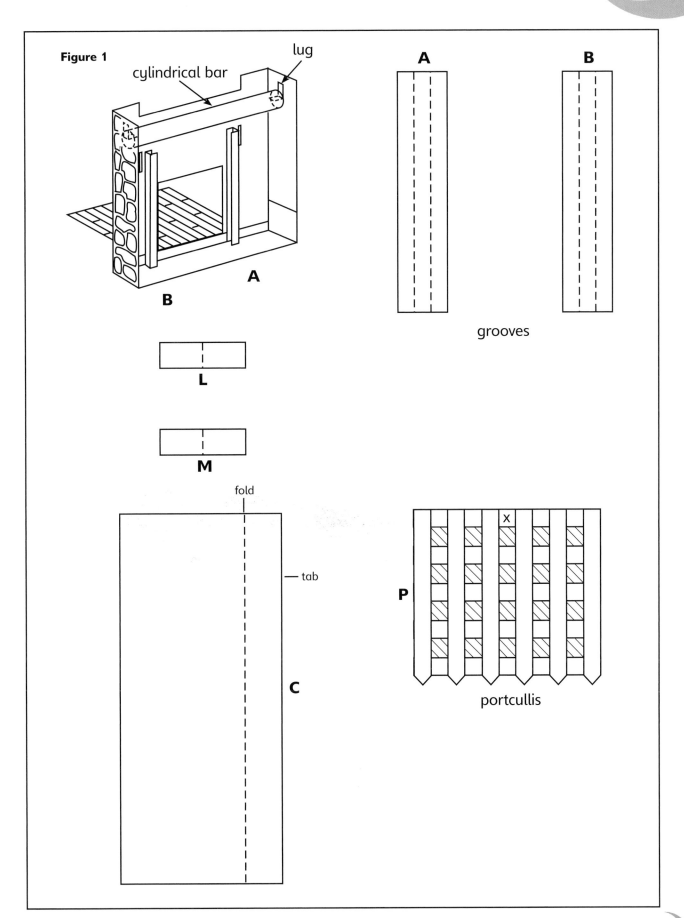

Figure 1

lug

cylindrical bar

A

B

grooves

L

M

fold

tab

C

x

P

portcullis

Theme 2 Doors and murder holes

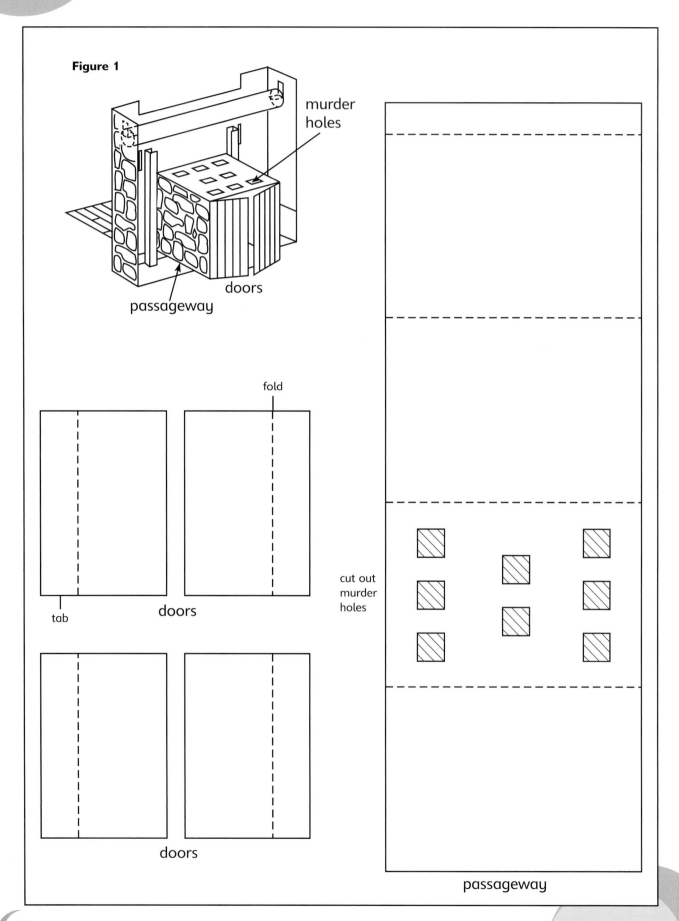

Figure 1

murder holes

passageway

doors

fold

doors

tab

cut out murder holes

doors

passageway

Walls and towers

BACKGROUND

Stonemasons built castles and identified their work with individual marks so that they could get paid. Castle walls could be up to 3.5m thick. The top of the wall was 'crenulated'. This means that it had raised walls called 'merlons', with gaps in between called 'crenels'. A merlon was about 1.5m wide and one to two metres high. A crenel was up to one metre wide. The slits in castle walls are called arrow loops and were used by archers and crossbowmen.

Spiral staircases were built to make people turn to the right as they came up them. This meant that right-handed soldiers could not strike at the defending soldiers with their swords, but the defending soldiers could attack. Wooden hoardings were built onto the crenellations in time of siege, allowing soldiers to drop missiles down the front of walls. In time, permanent crenellations were built which over-hung the front of the wall and these were called 'machicolations'.

THE CONTENTS
Lesson 1 (Ages 5–7)
Castle walls

The children cut out a wall and walkway, giving the outer wall a stone effect and mason's marks. They can attach the walls to the gatehouse they made in Theme 2.

Lesson 2 (Ages 7–9)
Towers

The children create a wall and a walkway, then a tower and watchtower. They can assemble a series of walls and towers to form an enclosure in which to place the keep from Theme 4 Lesson 2.

Lesson 3 (Ages 9–11)
Hoardings and machicolations

The children assemble a tower and make hoardings to cover the top. They learn how machicolations developed from hoardings.

Notes on photocopiables
Curtain wall (page 30)

This sheet features a section of a curtain wall. The blank side acts as the outer wall and can have stones drawn on it. The printed side shows the position of the walkway and the lugs to support it. Children glue a walkway along the dotted line on the wall and attach the lugs to support it. Pictures show the completed wall, with mason's marks indicated by $\times$, Y and $\triangledown$.

Towers (page 31)

Children will need two copies of this sheet to make all four tower walls, roof and a base.

Hoardings and machicolations (page 32)

The letters on the Hoarding (1) identify the following parts: A is the floor which rests on the tower roof; B is the back wall; C is the roof; D is the wall overhanging the tower floor in front of the wall; and E shows the base and the holes for dropping things on attackers. Hoarding (1) is folded and positioned on the tower as shown in Figure 1. The second template, Hoarding (2), can be made to fit on either side of the first one, but one or both hoardings may need to be cut to make them fit. Figure 2 shows an example of how the machicolations looked on the tower.

IMAGE EUBUILDIT PROJECT WARWICK UNIVERSITY HTTP://WWW.EUBUILDIT.NET © SEAN NEILL

Lesson 1 Castle walls

Resources and preparation
● Make copies of page 30, 'Curtain wall', one for each child.
● Provide glue and scissors for each child or small group of children.

What to do
● Explain to the children that they are going to build a model castle, beginning by making some walls. Give each child a copy of the photocopiable sheet and point out the two pictures showing how the inside of the wall will look with its walkway for soldiers, and how the front will look when stones have been drawn in.
● Invite the children to 'become' stonemasons who have to work together to build a castle, using individual marks to identify their work. Ask groups of two or three children to divide up different parts of the wall so that they can all draw stones onto it. Remember to tell them to draw on the blank side of the wall (the printed side shows a dotted line for positioning the inner walkway). Each child should devise a simple mark on rough paper and then make a small copy of it on the first and last stone they draw.
● Instruct the children to cut out the walkway supports A, B and C, and the walkway D, for later use.
● Ask them to cut out the wall ('E') next. Some children may need help cutting out the crenellations. Alternatively they could draw a horizontal line across each crenel in line with the tops of the merlons and shade in the gaps to represent wooden shutters.

● Direct the children to fold the tab on the walkway and glue it under the dotted line on the wall.
● Ask the children to fold each walkway support along the dotted line and to glue them on both sides in order to position them on the places indicated on the wall.
● Finally, see if the children can get their castle walls to stand up. Sections of wall could be glued together, or left to attach to the towers that can be made in Lesson 2 in this theme.

Extension
● Having made the model walls, encourage the children to consider the actual sizes of walls by measuring the thickness of a wall in school and measuring out 3.5m to show the thickness of a castle wall. Challenge them to measure out the size of two merlons, each 1.5m wide by 2m high, perhaps chalking them out on the playground and marking a 1m gap for the crenel between them.
● They could also try making crenellations out of the largest pieces of cardboard they can find and then compare them with the crenellations they have marked out.

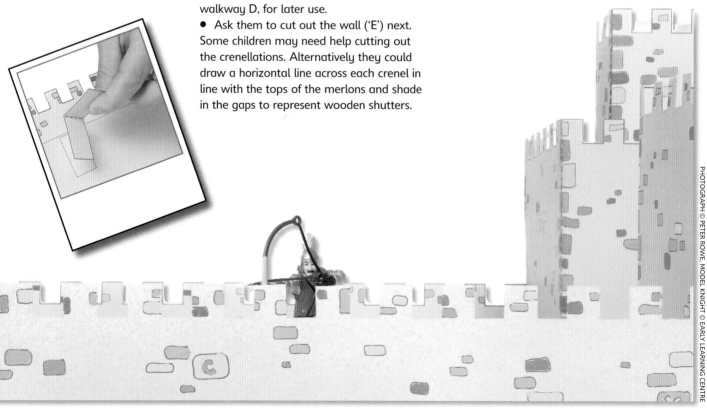

Lesson 2 Towers

Resources and preparation

● Make one copy page 30, 'Curtain wall', and two copies of page 31, 'Towers',for each child.
● You will need glue and scissors for each child or small group of children.

Starter

● Remind the children that the first castles had walls made of wood but these could be easily burned down and so later castles were built of stone to make them fireproof. Tell the children that they are going to make the outer defences of a model castle starting with the walls.
● Distribute the 'Curtain wall' photocopiable sheet and show the children the picture of the outer wall with the stones, while talking about stonemasons and their individual marks. (If you have time show them how to draw in the stones as explained in Lesson 1). Explain the second picture which shows their model wall will look from the inside of the castle grounds, then let them cut out the wall and assemble it. Point out that the walkway (D) is glued in place before the supports (A, B and C).

What to do

● When the children have completed the walls, explain the role of the towers in providing a higher platform that could be used as look-out points, enabling better defence of the walls.
● Give each child two copies of the 'Towers' photocopiable sheet and ask them to look at the picture of the tower and watch tower in Figure 1. Notice how the tower can be joined to the curtain walls. A tower can also be used to make a corner of the castle with two walls joined at right angles.
● Challenge the children to cut out two sets of walls and stick them together to make the main tower. The roof/base template on one sheet can be used as a base or floor, and on the second sheet can be used for the roof on which the small watchtower will be placed. The dashed lines mark the place where the roof should be attached.
● Next ask the children to cut out and make the watchtower – again, using two sets of walls from both sheets.
● Finally, see if the children can successfully assemble a main tower with a smaller watchtower positioned on top.

AGES 7–9

Objectives
● To assemble a castle wall and walkway.
● To assemble a tower and join it to a wall.

Subject references
Design and technology
● Generate ideas for products after thinking about who will use them.
(NC: KS2 1a)
● Cut and shape a range of materials, and assemble, join and combine components and materials accurately.
(NC: KS2 2d)

ILLUSTRATION © LASZLO VERES/BEEHIVE ILLUSTRATION

Differentiation

• Give less confident learners the opportunity to make both walls and towers with support, either from an adult or by pairing them with a more confident learner. They could be put in charge of making the simpler watchtowers.

• Extend children by challenging them to work out a plan for a castle, using guidebooks to help them. Encourage them to assemble the walls and towers (and the gatehouse from Theme 2) in different ways and to ask the class which design they think is the best.

Assessment

The children can be assessed on the standard of their walls and towers.

Plenary

• Invite the children to consider how to arrange the walls and towers into a castle's outer defences. They could look at the arrangements provided by the more confident learners (see Differentiation) or the whole class could work together to invent and try out different designs.

• Encourage the children to explain why they have selected a feature and positioned it in a certain way. For example, they may have planned a tower to go with every wall section to give better defence.

Outcomes

• The children can make a model of a castle wall with towers.

• The children see that castle builders had problems with design just as engineers have design problems with buildings today.

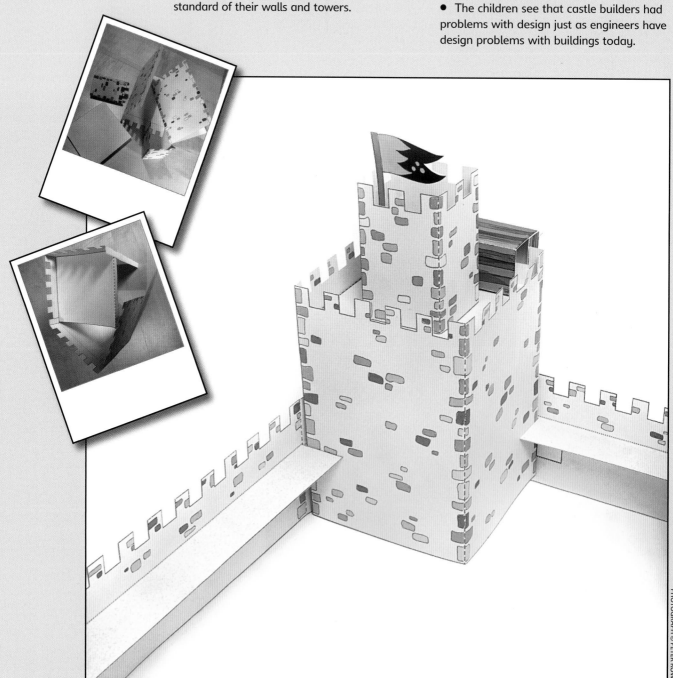

HOT TOPICS Castles

Lesson 3 Hoardings and machicolations

PHOTOGRAPH © PETER ROWE

AGES 9–11

Objectives
● To assemble a tower.
● To assemble a hoarding and attach it to a tower.
● To work out a way of attaching a second hoarding to a tower.

Subject references
Design and technology
● Develop ideas and explain them clearly. (NC: KS2 1b)
● Plan what they have to do, suggesting a sequence of actions and alternatives, if needed. (NC: KS2 1c)
● Cut and shape a range of materials, and assemble, join and combine components and materials accurately. (NC: KS2 2d)

Resources and preparation
● Make two copies of page 31, 'Towers', and one copy of page 32, 'Hoardings and machicolations', for each child.
● Provide glue and scissors for each child or small group of children.

What to do
● Explain to the children they are going to make a model tower and a device that protects it from attack.
● Give them two copies of the 'Towers' photocopiable sheet and encourage them to make a tower, using the instructions from Lesson 2. They do not need to make and use the watchtower in this activity.
● When the children have made their towers, tell them that when an enemy attacked a castle wall, they tried to set up a fire to destroy the mortar holding the stones together or they tried to hack out the stones from the wall. Archers could not fire down on them from their arrow loops and soldiers hanging over the wall could be easily shot by the enemy archers. One way of dealing with the wall destroyers was to build hoardings before the battle, which were used as explained in the Background information section (see page 25).
● Hand out the 'Hoardings and machicolations' photocopiable sheet. Ask the children to look at how the hoarding fits

over the tower as shown in Figure 1. Explain that you would like them to assemble a hoarding onto the tower. Look in Notes on photocopiables (see page 25) to identify parts A to E.
● Show the children how to fold parts A to E of the hoarding so that it fits over the tower. They should glue the inner base to the tower roof and glue the tab alongside part E to the outer tower wall. Explain that it should look like a box, except the bottom of the hoarding will fold outwards, so it rests away from the tower.
● Invite the children to display their finished towers and hoardings together.

Extension
● Challenge the children to cut out the second hoarding unit and set it up at right angles to the first on the top of the tower so that two walls are protected. The children may have to cut pieces away in both hoardings to make them fit.
● If the children have been making a model castle, they could try to design hoardings to go over the walkway of the curtain walls (see Lesson 1 in this theme). This could involve using the hoarding template and working by trial and error to amend it to fit the curtain walls.

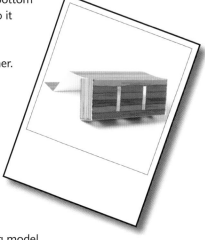

Theme 3 Curtain wall

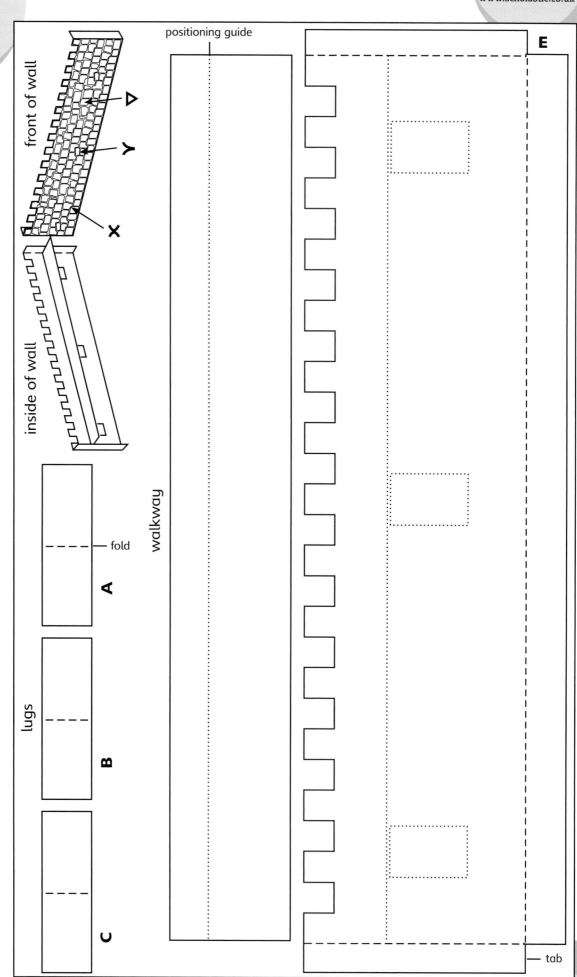

front of wall

inside of wall

walkway

positioning guide

fold

A

lugs

B

C

E

tab

Theme 3 Towers

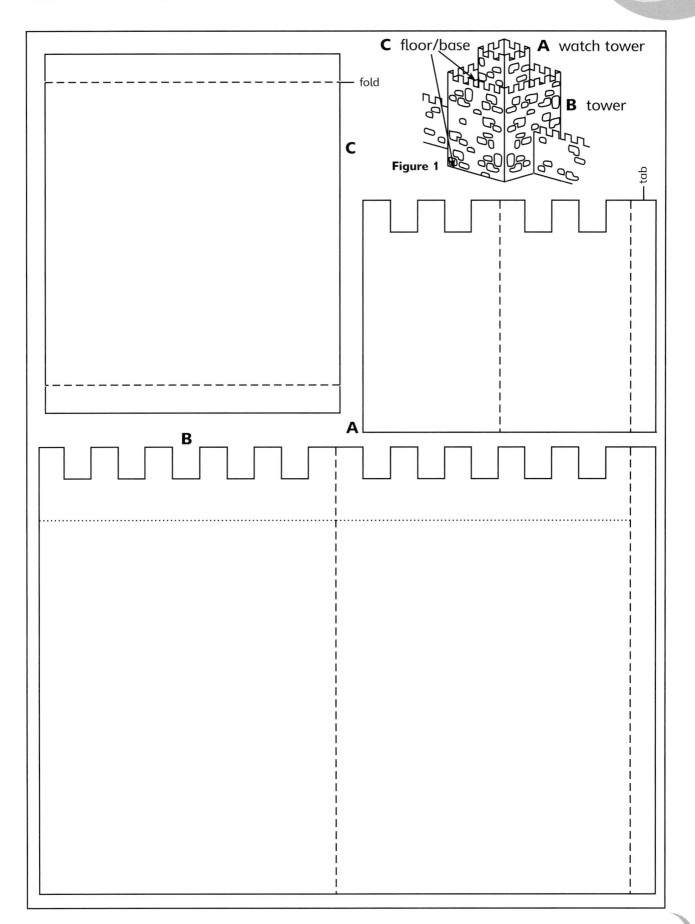

C floor/base   A watch tower

B tower

Figure 1

fold

C

A

B

tab

Theme 3 Hoardings and machicolations

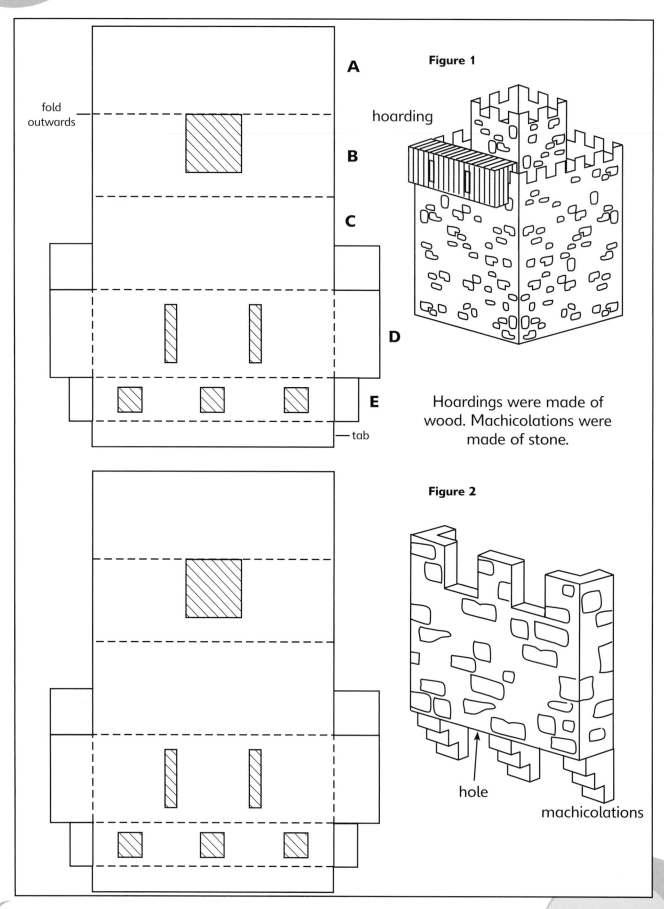

A

B

C

D

E

fold outwards

tab

Figure 1

hoarding

Hoardings were made of wood. Machicolations were made of stone.

Figure 2

hole

machicolations

Inside the castle walls

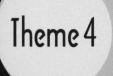

BACKGROUND

This theme focuses on the people, then buildings, within a castle. People who lived in castles are introduced in Lesson 1, making a change from the buildings element concentrated on so far. However, you could leave Lesson 1 until you get to Theme 6 'Castle Life'.

The lord governed his castle and lands. A constable or castellan ran the castle, and a steward was employed to maintain the lands. The lord's wife, a lady, had a lady-in-waiting and other maids, and also nurses for her children. Page boys performed general duties, heralds took messages, and the knights fought for their lord. A chaplain held religious services for the people within the castle and other 'castle people' included a cook, brewer, carpenter, blacksmith, armourer and groom.

The keep had three to five floors and was the home of the lord, his family, and his knights. Access to the keep was through a door on the first floor, arranged to make it difficult to use a battering ram to break it down. A trapdoor led from the first floor to the ground floor, and this used as a food store or a dungeon. The Great Hall was also on the first floor, where magnificent and impressive feasts were held. The solar, on the second floor, was the family bedroom.

THE CONTENTS
Lesson 1 (Ages 5–7)
Castle people
The children identify ten people who live in the castle and cut out a knight and four soldiers, positioning them around the castle walls, discussing their reasoning. The pictures of medieval costumes can be used as a stimulus for what to wear on your Castle Day.

Lesson 2 (Ages 7–9)
The keep
The children make a keep from a shoebox using materials of their choice and a diagram on the photocopiable sheet to guide them.

Lesson 3 (Ages 9–11)
Castle buildings
The children study the site plan of a hypothetical castle, which shows many features, and use an internet site to compare it to real site plans of castles.

Notes on photocopiables
Castle people (page 38)
This sheet has pictures of ten people who live in a castle with their names listed in boxes. The children cut out the pictures and names and match them up. The answers are: A) knight, B) lady, C) blacksmith, D) chaplain, E) lady-in-waiting, F) lord, G) steward, H) groom, I) constable, J) cook. There is a knight and four soldiers to cut out and place on the castle models from previous lessons.

Making a keep (page 39)
This sheet shows how a shoebox can be made into a model keep.

A castle and site plan (page 40)
This sheet depicts a castle and site plan, allowing the children to relate the plan details to the picture features. The children have to find the missing well from the site plan and draw it in.

Lesson 1 Castle people

AGES 5–7

Objectives
● To learn the names of the different people who lived in a castle and to know about their work.

Subject references
History
● Identify differences between ways of life at different times. (NC: KS1 2b)
Art and design
● Investigate the possibilities of a range of materials and processes. (NC: KS1 2a)
● Understand visual and tactile elements including colour, pattern and texture. (NC: KS1 4a)

Resources and preparation
● Photocopy page 38, 'Castle people', one for each child.
● You will need the model gatehouse, wall and towers from Themes 2 and 3. Insert a square piece of card or paper in the very top of the watchtower so that soldiers can stand on it.
● Provide a selection of different fabrics and materials (optional), and information books showing costumes from the 11th to the 14th century. Ideas for clothes can also be found at the following websites: **www.lothene.demon.co.uk/crafts6.html** and **www.medieval-banquet.co.uk**
● This lesson can be adapted to be part of your Castle Day.

What to do
● Ask the children who they think lived in castles. Show them the pictures on the 'Castle people' sheet and tell them about the people who live in a castle. Use the information in the Background section (see page 33), but do not refer to any person on the sheet in particular.
● Challenge the children to cut out the people and the names and try to match them up.

● Point out the different types of clothes worn by the people in the castle. If you have a selection of fabrics, pass them round and ask who might have worn such materials. As a general rule, drab colours of brown and grey were worn by poor people and bright colours of red and blue were worn by rich people. The people marked C, H and J would have worn drab colours.
● Display colour pictures of castle people from books or the internet (copyright permitting) and say that for Castle Day they can dress up as anyone they please (be prepared for lots of knights and ladies). Send a letter home explaining this aim and encourage parents and carers to help. If you feel that some children will not be able to bring a costume, gather together some items that they could use.
● If you have made the castle models in Themes 2 and 3, invite the children to imagine that each one of them is a knight and has four soldiers to command. Encourage them to cut out the knight and soldiers and place them on their models. Can they give reasons for the positions they have adopted? Look for answers such as guarding the gateway, watching out for enemies and so on.

Extension
● Give out copies of page 40, 'A castle and a site plan', and talk about the buildings in the upper picture. Explain that the constable lived in the gatehouse to keep a close watch on who entered and left the castle, and that people such as the cook, groom and blacksmith slept close to where they worked, while the lord and lady had their own bedroom.
● Invite the children to share their ideas on what they think it was like to live in a castle. Keep a record of their responses to compare with responses after they have finished the topic.

ILLUSTRATION © LASZLO VERES/BEEHIVE ILLUSTRATION

HOT TOPICS Castles

Lesson 2 The keep

ROCHESTER CASTLE © MEDWAY COUNCIL

AGES 7–9

Objectives
● To use a range of materials and processes to construct a model keep.

Subject references
Design and technology
● Develop ideas and explain them clearly, putting together a list of what they want their design to achieve. (NC: KS2 1b)
● Select appropriate tools and techniques for making their product. (NC: KS2 2a)
● Measure, mark out, cut and shape a range of materials and assemble, join and combine components and materials accurately. (NC: KS2 2d)
● Reflect on the progress of their work as they design and make, identifying ways they could improve their product. (NC: KS2 3a)

Resources and preparation
● Make copies of page 39, 'Making a keep'.
● You will need the following for each child or group: shoe box, plastic straws, lump of Plasticine, pieces of card, cardboard tube from kitchen roll, spent matches, scissors, sticky tape, ruler. For the outside steps, less confident learners could use wooden blocks or dominoes. More confident learners could use card to make steps.
● Provide information books showing castle keeps. A picture of Rochester castle keep could be used to generate interest. Visit **www.castleuk.net/castle_lists_south/ 178/rochestercastlepicture1.htm**
● This activity can be used as a competition for children aged nine to eleven on your Castle Day.

Starter
● Show the children the picture of an impressive castle keep and tell them that this was the home of the castle lord and his knights. Ask them to work out how many floors are in the keep. Tell them about the door being on the first floor to prevent the use of a battering ram.
● Explain that they are going to make a model keep, but unlike the other lessons so far, where they have cut out and assembled the castle features, they are now going to convert a shoebox into a keep. Note that

the shoebox has been selected because it is easy to collect, but the keep it makes is on a larger scale than the gatehouse, wall and towers. If you wish to make a keep at the same scale, you will need to select a box which is about 5cm taller than the tower with its watchtower.

What to do
● Give the children a copy of 'Making a keep'. Tell them that they are going to use a range of materials such as card, straws and matchsticks to make a keep.
● Let the children study the picture and decide how they are going to make the keep. If you feel they are competent to begin, let them start. If they need help, offer it by using the steps below.

Steps in making the keep
● The inside dimensions of the shoebox need to be measured to make the floors. The dimensions should be marked out on card and a little extra is needed to make the tabs, which are turned down to stick to the inside walls.
● Before the floors are fitted, the first floor needs to be cut to create a trapdoor. One side of the door could be left uncut and then folded so that it acts like a working trapdoor. (This would work even better if a small tab were attached to act as a handle.)

- Ask the children to decide upon the height of the first floor in the keep and stick it in place.
- Make a fireplace out of Plasticine, with one or more straws for a flue and chimney. Cut a hole in the top of the keep for the chimney. (If you prefer, details like the fireplace could be drawn onto the walls instead.)
- Place a cardboard tube (for the staircase) in the corner and cut it down to make it fit. Cut two doorways into the stairs for the first and second floors. (An easier alternative would be to paint the doorways on.)
- Next, the children cut a hole into the second floor to accommodate the straw flue and the staircase.
- Once all the holes have been matched up, stick the tube, then the second floor, into place.
- Make a second Plasticine fireplace and straw flue, and add these.
- Create a ladder from two long thin pieces of card and spent matchsticks. Position it below the trapdoor.

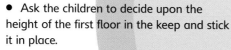

- A front for the keep can be made from the shoebox lid or piece of card. Cut out a door and windows and stick the front loosely into place, using sticky tape, so that it can be opened or closed for viewing.
- Crenellations cut from card, can be added to the top.
- Add steps in front of the outer door and erect a flag made from paper, supported by a straw pole.

Differentiation
- Ask less confident learners to put in the floors, the trapdoor and upper fireplace.
- Invite more confident learners to look at castle furniture and to create some for the keep.

Assessment
The quality of work can be assessed along with how much help was needed. Many children will need some assistance as this is a big project.

Plenary
Conclude the lesson by asking the children how they found the building activity. They may have realised that it is quite complicated and you could ask them to imagine what it was like for the designers, stonemasons and carpenters who built keeps in real life, hundreds of years ago.

Outcome
The children can use a range of skills to make a castle keep.

PHOTOGRAPH © ANDREA LEWIS

HOT TOPICS Castles

Lesson 3 Castle buildings

Resources and preparation
● Make copies of 'A castle and site plan', one for each child.
● You will need computer access for each child or group to use the following websites about castles in Wales (**www.greatcastles ofwales.co.uk/castles_index.htm**) and in the United Kingdom (**www.castleuk.net/ main_map_page.htm**).

What to do
● Remind the children about the features of castles they have made in other lessons and give them a copy of the photocopiable sheet.
● Together, look at the picture of a typical castle on the sheet. Talk them through the various buildings featured using the Background information (see page 33).
● Start with the keep and say how it was the home of the lord and his knights, and contained a Great Hall, solar (bedroom) and chapel. Explain that as the castle developed, special buildings were erected for these features as the keep was found to be too cold and uncomfortable. Remind the children that a key feature of a castle was a well.
● Say that few castles remain intact today and that in many ruins, only the outlines of the buildings are seen in the foundations.

From these archaeologists have made site plans.
● Ask the children to label the site plan using the picture to help them. Tell them that one feature is missing from the site plan and challenge them to find it and draw it in. (The well is missing.)
● Encourage the children to access the websites and look for site plans of the castles featured. (Most castles on the websites have them.)
● Invite the children to compare their site plan with the site plans of other castles and make a report.

Extension
● Explain to the children that castles were erected near important roads and rivers, or where roads met. This was done so that the lord and his knights could control them.
● Challenge them to use the internet to find castles in their local area or an area where they have been on holiday and look at the castles and their maps. When they click on the castle map of an area they will see which castles were near roads, rivers or both. The maps that show recent roads and reference to motorways may not be relevant, but major roads and even minor ones may have existed in the time the castle was built.

great hall

curtain wall

gate house

barbican

motte and bailey from earlier castle

tower with machicolations at the top

PHOTOGRAPH © WARWICK CASTLE

Theme 4 Castle people

A
B
C
D
E

F
G
H
I
J

| chaplain | lady-in-waiting | cook | blacksmith | steward |
| knight | lady | groom | constable | lord |

Theme 4 **Making a keep**

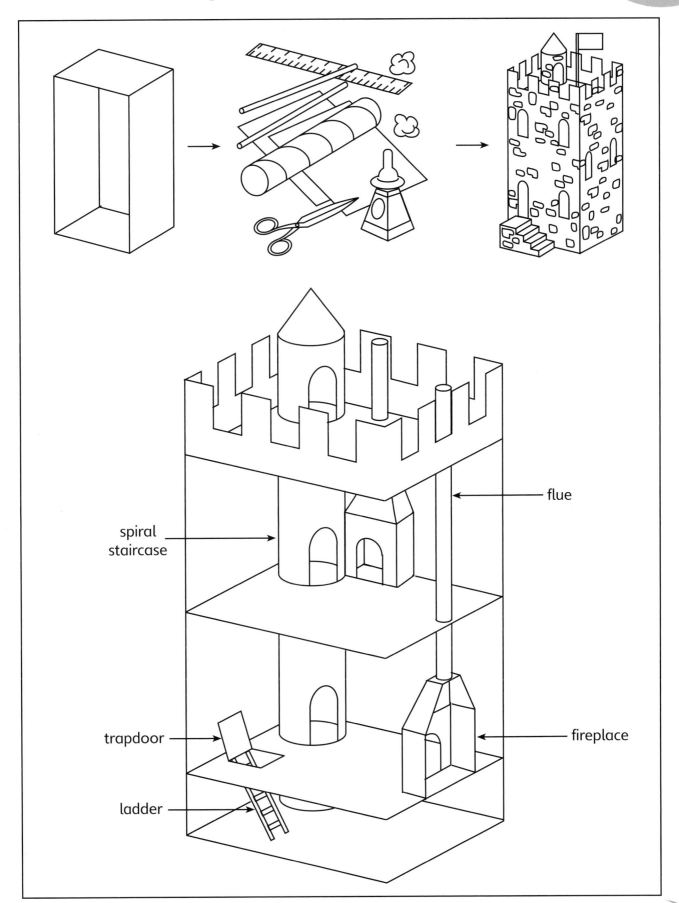

spiral staircase

flue

trapdoor

fireplace

ladder

Theme 4 A castle and site plan

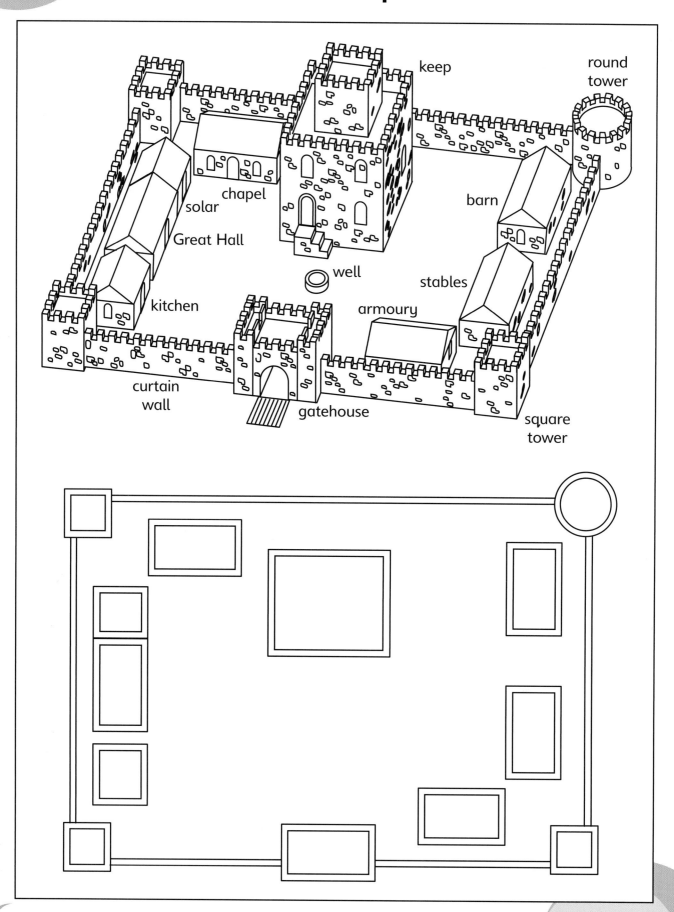

Knights

BACKGROUND

Heraldry was devised so that a knight could be identified on the battlefield. There were basic designs of shields such as bend, chief, cross, fesse and pale, and subdivisions of these designs. (See Notes on photocopiables: Heraldry (page 46), below.) The badge of a knight could also feature an animal such as a bird or lion, and it was also used on the surcoat (a coat covering the suit of armour), the trapper (the cloth covering the horse) and the banner. The banner was used by a lord (who was also a knight) to show his knights where he was fighting on the battlefield.

The colours used in heraldry are silver, (argent), gold or red (glues), blue (azure), green, (vert), purple (purpur) and black (sable). The crest is an ornament on the helmet. The coat of arms features the shield, helmet and crest and two objects (often animals or people) called supporters on either side of the shield.

THE CONTENTS
Lesson 1 (Ages 5–7)
Heraldry

The children look at shield designs and how they are repeated throughout a knight's costume. They learn that the crest is a decoration on the helmet and see how the shield, crest and supporters make up the coat of arms. They then create their own designs.

Lesson 2 (Ages 7–9)
Armour

The children make a model piece of chainmail and compare it with a diagram of a real piece of chainmail. They identify the components of a suit of armour and make parts of armour using Plasticine.

Lesson 3 (Ages 9–11)
The making of a knight

The children read a story about the various stages in the making of a knight. They can use the information as the basis of a play.

Notes on photocopiables
Heraldry (page 46)

This sheet depicts five basic charges: bend (top left); chief (below); pale (top right); fesse (below); cross (centre). The shields second, third and fourth from the left show variations on the bend and are known as per bend, bendy, and bend raguly. The three shields on the right of the cross are per pale indented, paly, and per pale. The blank knight and coat of arms are for the children to fill in.

Armour (page 47)

Figures 1, 2 and 3 show how to make a piece of model chain mail and a piece of real chain mail for comparison. Figure 4 shows the parts of a suit of armour and Figures 5, 6, 7 and 8 show how to add pieces of model armour to a Plasticine figure.

The making of a knight (page 48)

This sheet features a dialogue between two squires who are about to be knighted and can be used as the basis of a comprehension or a play.

The answers to the questions are:
Q1) Seven; Q2) Page boy; Q3) To make them strong; Q4) Run errands, serve meals, learn to read, write, sing and play chess; Q5) 14; Q6) Clean armour, helping put it on, look after horses; Q7) 21; Q8) He receives a sword and a pair of spurs, and is tapped on both shoulders while his lord says 'Arise sir...' .

PHOTOGRAPH © PETER ROWE, MODEL SHIELDS © EARLY LEARNING CENTRE

Lesson 1 Heraldry

Resources and preparation
● Photocopy page 46, 'Heraldry', for each child.
● Provide coloured pencils with yellow for gold, plus red, blue, green, purple and black.
● This lesson can be adapted to be part of your Castle Day.

What to do
● Ask the children what they know about knights and look for an answer about them wearing suits of armour.
● Invite them to imagine that they are all knights in suits of armour. How could they tell who was in each suit? Look for an answer about a badge or some similar method of identification, and tell the children about heraldry and how it helped knights identify each other.
● Give the children the photocopiable sheet and discuss the shield designs. You may wish to draw each one on the board and name it.
● At this point, introduce the colours used in heraldry and colour in some of the shields. The children could also select a shield design, draw it on paper and use any of the heraldic colours to colour it in.
● Return to the photocopiable sheet and discuss the arrangement

of the badge on the knight. Ask the children to think up a badge for themselves and draw it on the blank knight in all the relevant places. Let them use heraldic colours to colour it in.
● Ask the children to think up a crest for their helmets. Draw attention to the knight's crest in the picture: it is the two wings from his badge. This may help the children to design a crest. Alternatively they may design something that is not associated with the badge. Invite them to draw in their crests on the correct place on the sheet.
● Move on to the coat of arms and discuss how it is made up from the crest and the shield, and has supporters. Challenge the children make a coat of arms from the badges and crests they have used in the lower picture. Explain that the knight would have displayed his coat of arms in his castle, perhaps on the gatehouse or over a fireplace in the Great Hall.

Extension
Ask the children to reflect on what they have done and consider changing their coat of arms. They could make a large picture of their coat of arms (their original idea or modified) for display on the wall. If you are organising a Castle Day, mount them around the classroom which will have been turned into a Great Hall.

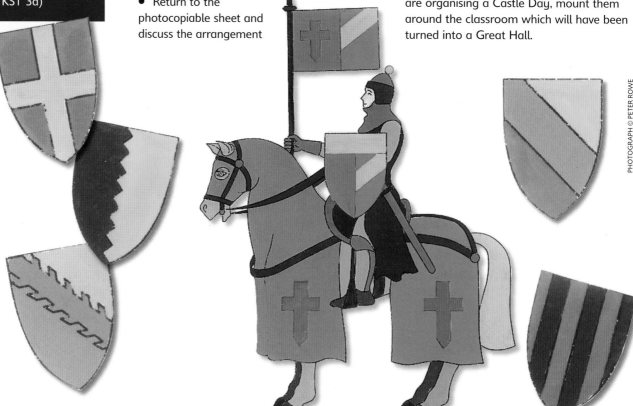

PHOTOGRAPH © PETER ROWE

Lesson 2 Armour

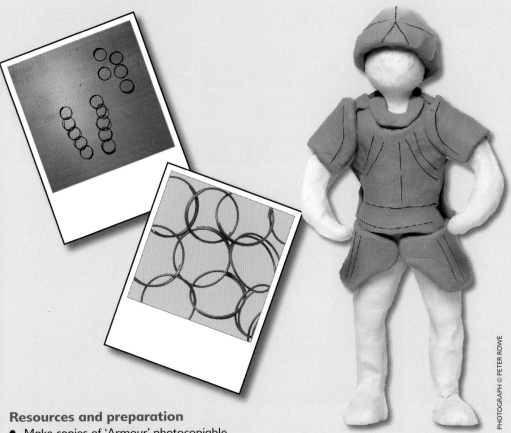

PHOTOGRAPH © PETER ROWE

Resources and preparation
● Make copies of 'Armour' photocopiable page 47 for every child.
● You will need a length of thin wire (about 30cm) such as that used for garden ties, scissors, large lump of yellow or white Plasticine for making the body of the knight, and large lump of grey Plasticine for making the armour, for each child or group.
● Provide information books showing pictures of knights in armour, especially chainmail.
● This lesson can be adapted to be part of your Castle Day.

Starter
● Show the children a picture of a knight with a suit of armour made mainly from chainmail. Tell them that the chainmail was made by linking rings of wire together.
● Hand out the photocopiable sheet, lengths of wire and scissors. Ask the children to make some wire rings about 1.5cm in diameter. (The rings do not have to be perfectly circular.) Encourage the children to make two columns of five rings as shown in Figure 1. Then ask them to make four more rings and link the columns together (see Figure 2). They should discover that the exercise requires great care and can be very time-consuming.

● Show the children Figure 3 and explain that in real chainmail, each ring links with four others and not with just two as they have made. From this they should realise that making chainmail is even more complicated than the activity they have performed.

What to do
● Together look at Figure 4 and point out the various parts of the armour. Discuss which parts of the body they protect. Tell the children that there was also a back plate which is similar in shape and size to the breastplate.
● Challenge the children to use the yellow or white Plasticine to make a model of a knight about 12cm high.
● Next, set about making armour from the grey Plasticine, using Figures 5 to 8 as a visual guide to help them. As the children are making the armour, tell them that knights were measured for their suits of armour so that the plates would fit correctly.
● Encourage the children to find the size of armour that fits best by going through a process of trial and error.

Differentiation
- Create rings for less confident learners so that they only have to link them together to make chainmail. They may need help in making the armour to the correct size for fitting on the knight.
- Extend children by challenging them to make more pieces of armour to cover the limbs and feet.

Assessment
The children can be assessed on the quality of their armour suits and their persistence in making their model chainmail.

Plenary
Ask the children what it would have been like to be an armourer in the day when most of the armour was chainmail. Can they imagine what it would have been like when suits of armour became popular? Explain that as the work was very time consuming, suits of armour became very expensive. The knights oftebused some of the money that their lands earned in rent to buy their suits.

Outcomes
- The children can make a simple model of chainmail and appreciate how the real chainmail was difficult to make.
- The children can make part of a model suit of armour.

Did you know?
Some suits of armour were not heavy. A knight could run in them.

Lesson 3 The making of a knight

Resources and preparation

● Photocopy page 48, 'The making of a knight', for each child.
● You will need a whiteboard and pens.
● This lesson can be adapted to be part of your Castle Day.

What to do

● Tell the children that they are going to find out how a boy became a knight. Let them know that they are going to do this by reading a conversation between two young men who are about to be knighted.
● Write these questions on the board for the children to answer:
 Q1 How old was a boy when the began training to be a knight?
 Q2 What was a boy training to be a knight called?
 Q3 Why did the boys wrestle and play tag?
 Q4 What else did the boys do?
 Q5 At what age did a boy become a squire?
 Q6 What were a squire's duties?
 Q7 At what age could a squire become a knight?
 Q8 What happened when a squire became a knight?
● Ask the children to read the text on the photocopiable sheet. When they have finished, discuss the questions and ask them to give you their answers. Write the answers on the board.
● Extend the children's thinking by asking if any of them would have liked to have become a knight if they lived in this time period. What do they think would have been the advantages and disadvantages of being a knight?

PHOTOGRAPH © WARWICK CASTLE

Extension

● If you are making the story into a short play, you will need costumes, three wooden swords and two pairs of spurs (made from pipe cleaners). Use the photocopiable sheet as a playscript and recruit actors to be Thomas, Robert, Lord Percival and two squires.
● You could use flashbacks and develop short playlets to involve more children. For example, show Thomas and Robert as page boys and as squires, or introduce Lady Eleanor, Father Benedict and Sir Geofrey and even his horse! This could be performed at the Castle Day in the infant school.

AGES 9–11

Objectives
● To understand the process of turning a boy into a knight.
● To extract information from a text.
● To express the information as a short play.

Subject references
English
● Use character, action and narrative to convey a story.
(NC: KS2 En1 4b)
● Obtain specific information through detailed reading.
(NC: KS2 En2 3c)
● Playscripts.
(NC: KS3 En2 8g)

PHOTOGRAPH © PETER ROWE. MODEL KNIGHTS © EARLY LEARNING CENTRE

Theme 5 **Heraldry**

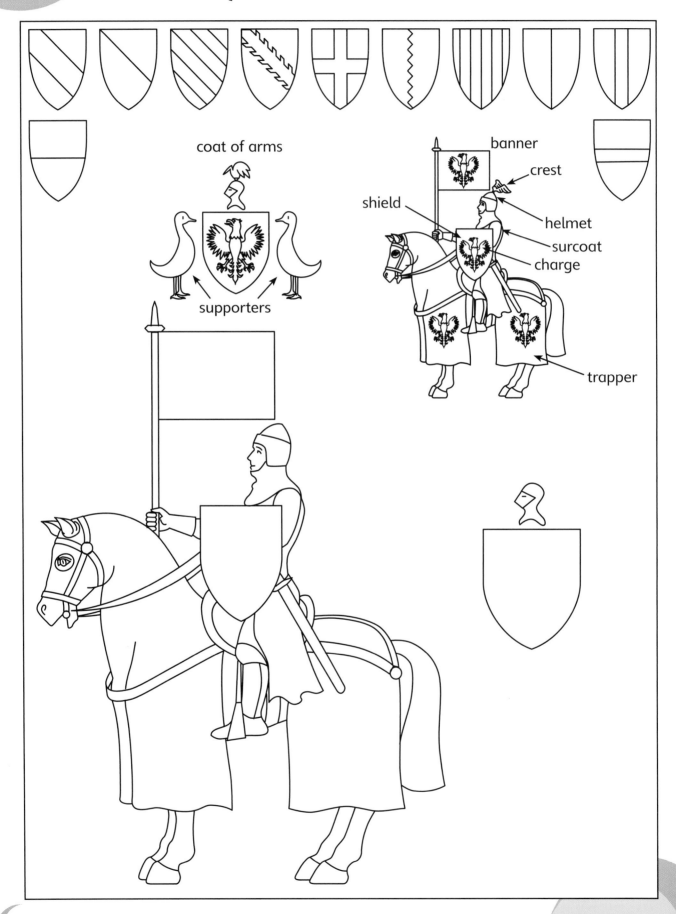

coat of arms

supporters

banner

crest

shield

helmet

surcoat

charge

trapper

Theme 5 Armour

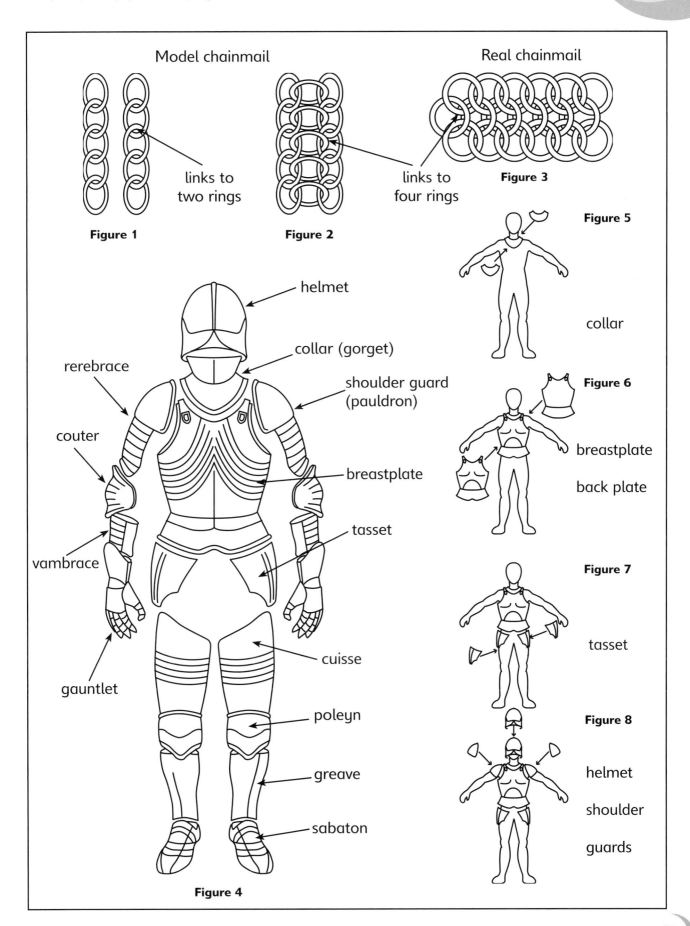

Model chainmail

links to two rings

Figure 1

links to four rings

Figure 2

Real chainmail

Figure 3

Figure 5

collar

Figure 6

breastplate

back plate

Figure 7

tasset

Figure 8

helmet

shoulder

guards

helmet

collar (gorget)

shoulder guard (pauldron)

rerebrace

couter

breastplate

vambrace

tasset

cuisse

gauntlet

poleyn

greave

sabaton

Figure 4

■SCHOLASTIC
www.scholastic.co.uk

Theme 5 The making of a knight

Robert and Tom are sat outside the Great Hall.

Robert: It was cold in the chapel last night.

Tom: Yes, but at least it kept me awake so I could keep praying. I spent the whole night laid flat out on my stomach.

Robert: Do you remember when we came to the castle?

Tom: We were only seven years old. I was very upset at leaving home.

Robert: Running all those errands for Lady Eleanor and serving meals.

Tom: Well, that's what page boys do.

Robert: And learn to read and write. Who was that first priest who taught us?

Tom: Father Benedict. He also taught us to sing. He taught me to play chess.

Robert: That's right, but I liked it better when we were 14 and became squires.

Tom: There was some good fun before that when we learned to ride, and played tag and wrestled to make us strong.

Robert: But learning to use the lance and the swords was the best.

Tom: I didn't like having to clean Sir Geofrey's armour and help him put it on.

Robert: Looking after Sir Leonard's horses was good but you had to watch Valiant. He could give you a nasty bite.

Tom: I'm glad we're 21 now and can become knights. Look! Here come the spurs and swords.

Two squires arrive each carrying a sword and a pair of spurs. One squire gives Tom his sword and Tom puts it in his belt. The squire then attaches spurs to his shoes. Robert also receives his sword and spurs. Robert and Tom go through to the Great Hall and Tom kneels before Lord Percival.

The Lord taps Tom on both shoulders:

The Lord: Arise Sir Thomas.

Sir Thomas steps aside so that Robert can be knighted as well.

Castle life

BACKGROUND

When the lord was away, he took most of his retinue with him. When he was present there were tournaments, music, dancing and feasting. These are the subjects of the next three lessons.

A major feature of a tournament was jousting, which saw knights charging at one another over an area called the 'lists'. Musical instruments played in medieval times included the recorder, cornet (a wooden trumpet), flute, sackbut (an early type of trombone), drums, mandolin, lute and hurdy-gurdy. A feature of medieval music was the drone. This was one or more notes played continuously throughout the piece of music.

When dining, people used a piece of stale bread, called a trencher, as a plate. When the meal was finished, scraps of food would be left on the trencher and gravy and sauces would have soaked into it. These trenchers were taken from the feast and given to the poor.

THE CONTENTS
Lesson 1 (Ages 5–7)
Jousting

The children make and use model knights in a jousting match to gain a little insight into what it was like to compete.

Lesson 2 (Ages 7–9)
Music and dance

The children learn to play a medieval song and perform a dance to go with it.

Lesson 3 (Ages 9–11)
Preparing a feast

The children find out about medieval feasts and work together to organise one.

Notes on photocopiables
Jousting (page 54)

Children glue this sheet onto card, cut out the horse and knight, and make a hole for the lance.

Castle Dance – The music (page 55)

This music is in the style of the medieval era. It is a simple 10-bar piece with a melody line for descant recorder, with two descant recorders providing a drone, and a drum providing the rhythm. If this instrumentation is unavailable then the melody and drone can be played on the piano, with the drone being played an octave lower.

Descant 1: This is an easy melody line that requires basic competency on the recorder. **Descants 2 and 3:** Children with no previous experience of recorder playing could be shown the fingerings for notes G and D and learn how to hold the note for two beats. **Drum:** The rhythm should be strongly maintained throughout with emphasis on the first beat. Sometimes when children play a repeating pattern or rhythm, there can be a tendency for the pulse to drift. To help avoid this the whole class could clap the rhythms. The importance of this line should be emphasised: without a strong beat the dance would descend into chaos!

Castle Dance – The dance (page 56)

Instructions are given for a simple dance in medieval style for the children to learn and perform. There are three diagrams to help the children visualise the dance.

There is no photocopiable for Lesson 3.

PHOTOGRAPH © WARWICK CASTLE

Lesson 1 Jousting

AGES 5–7

Objectives
● To let the children see what knights did when jousting.
● To appreciate that materials became worn in jousting.

Subject references
Science
● Find out about, and describe the movement of, familiar things.
(NC: KS1 Sc4 2a)
● Pushes are examples of forces.
(NC: KS1 Sc4 2b)
History
● Learn about the way of life of people in the more distant past who lived in the local area or elsewhere in Britain.
(NC: KS1 6b)
Mathematics
● Measure objects using uniform non-standard units, then with a standard unit of length.
(NC: KS1 Ma3 4a)
Design and technology
● Measure, mark out and cut a range of materials.
(NC: KS1 2c)

Resources and preparation
● Photocopy the 'Jousting' photocopiable onto card (page 54).
● You will need scissors, plastic straws, rulers, felt-tipped pens for each child, and small lumps of Plasticine.
● This lesson can be adapted to be part of your Castle Day.

What to do
● Tell the children about jousting tournaments using the information in the Background section to help you (page 49).
● Give each child the 'Jousting' sheet that has been copied or glued onto card. Let them look at the jousting knights. Explain that they are going to prepare a knight for jousting.
● Ask the children to cut out the knight and horse, or have them prepared beforehand. Cut the hole for the lance yourself.
● Next, the children should fold the card horse along line CD to make it stand up.
● Then they should cut along the line AB on the knight. Ask them to bend the knight's left leg a little further forward than the right leg, so that when the knight is slotted on to his horse, he turns a little to the left.
● Give out straws, a ruler, felt-tipped pens and a pair of scissors and challenge the

children to make a 10cm long lance by marking out the correct length and cutting it.
● Invite the children to insert the lance into the hole on the knight so that about 3cm sticks out at the back. The lance should pass over the left shoulder of the horse.
● When they are ready, announce the beginning of a jousting competition! Direct the children to gently move each knight towards the other so that their lances touch and note what happens. A knight is pushed over a little; he is pushed off or just receives a glancing blow.
● After a number of charges are made, the children may realise that the knight and lance need extra support. Point out that the lances become worn after a while. Why do they think this is?
● Encourage the children to experiment with making a small Plasticine saddle and also plasticine to hold the lance in its hole. *Which designs work best for jousting?*

Extension
If the children have done the lesson on heraldry (Theme 5 Lesson 1), they can decorate the knight and horse in the same heraldic devices as before or choose new ones.

Lesson 2 Music and dance

THE TROUBADOURS WWW.ANCESTRAL.CO.UK © VALERIE MARSHALL

Resources and preparation
● Make copies of both 'Castle Dance' photocopiables (pages 55 and 56).
● You will need recorders or piano, drums and a wooden recorder.
● This lesson can be adapted to be part of your Castle Day.

Starter
● Ask the children to name different types of musical instrument. Tell them about the instruments in medieval times using the information in the Background section to help (see page 49). Show them a recorder and say that present day recorders are very similar to the ones used in medieval times, and then reveal the wooden recorder. Explain to the children that in those times recorders were made of wood, but today many are made of plastic.
● Ask the children if they know any dances and invite them to demonstrate. Tell them they are going to learn a simple dance like the ones people danced in medieval times.

What to do
● The way in which this activity develops will depend on resources. If you have some children who are competent on recorders, give them the 'Castle Dance' music sheet before the lesson so that they can learn it.
● If you do not have any recorder players, enlist the help of someone who can play the piano. All the children can learn to keep the rhythm by clapping or beating drums.
● Practise the music for the castle dance until all of the children can join in with the clapping, beating of the drum, or can play the music on recorders competently.
● Next, hand out the dance photocopiable sheet and slowly go through all the stages of the dance. Encourage the children to practise and, once they are comfortable with it and know all of the moves, they can perform the dance to the music for the Plenary.
● If you are having a Castle Day, invite the children to perform the dance and music to the rest of the school.

Differentiation
- Less confident learners can beat the rhythm with a selection of percussion instruments or play the drone line.
- Encourage more confident learners to devise extra steps for the dance to perform with a second repeat of the music.

Assessment
The children can be assessed on the way they can keep a rhythm and how they learn a simple dance.

Plenary
Ask the recorder players to play the music while some of the class play the drums. Invite the rest of the class to perform the dance to the music.

Outcomes
- The children can keep a rhythm in a piece of music.
- The children can learn and perform a dance.

Did you know?
Minstrels (musicians), singers, storytellers, poets and a jester provided entertainment at a feast.

HOT TOPICS Castles

Lesson 3 Preparing a feast

Resources and preparation

• Provide information books about medieval life, which feature food and eating, especially about a feast in a Great Hall of a castle.

• You will need materials and objects to serve as the fireplace and to make tapestries to hang on the walls, clear plastic cups, plastic wineglasses, paper plates, plastic knives and spoons for the whole class, and salt, pepper and mustard.

• Ask the children to bring in packed meals featuring any of the following: roast beef slices, roast ham, roast chicken, boiled eggs, bread, meat pies, apple pies, jelly, blancmange, grape juice for wine (for wealthy), ginger beer for beer (for poor).

• If you are having a warm meal, Scotch broth is similar to pottage which everyone ate.

• Provide horn and trumpets (real or pretend).

• This lesson can be adapted to be part of your Castle Day.

PHOTOGRAPH © BRIAN SEED/ALAMY

What to do

• Tell the children that they are going to turn the classroom into a Great Hall in a castle and have a feast in it. Let them look through the range of information books to find out about how a feast was organised. Steer them towards the following points for your feast:

1) Classroom features – There needs to be a fireplace with the coat of arms of the lord (see Theme 5 Lesson 1). The table at which the lord and his family and friends sit needs to be close to the fireplace. Tables need to be long (smaller tables joined together) and chairs can be used instead of benches for seating.

2) For the meal – Set the tables with paper plates (for trenchers), clear plastic cups – glasses for the wealthy and plain plastic cups for the poor, plastic knives and spoons for each place setting (no forks). Add salt, pepper and mustard to the table.

3) For procedure – A child blows the horn to summon the diners and the wealthy diners sit down first. Then a group of children blow the trumpets as a fanfare to herald the arrival of the food. The poorer diners carry in the food and then seat themselves at the tables.

• When all the children are settled, choose a child to be the priest and say a grace. As the children eat their dinner, one child will need to be the cupbearer to make sure the lords on the table always have full glasses.

• Discuss the differences in the meal between the rich and the poor.

Extension

If the children have learned the play in Theme 5 Lesson 3, they could perform it before the feast, and use the feast as a celebration of the squires being knighted.

■SCHOLASTIC
www.scholastic.co.uk

Theme 6 Jousting

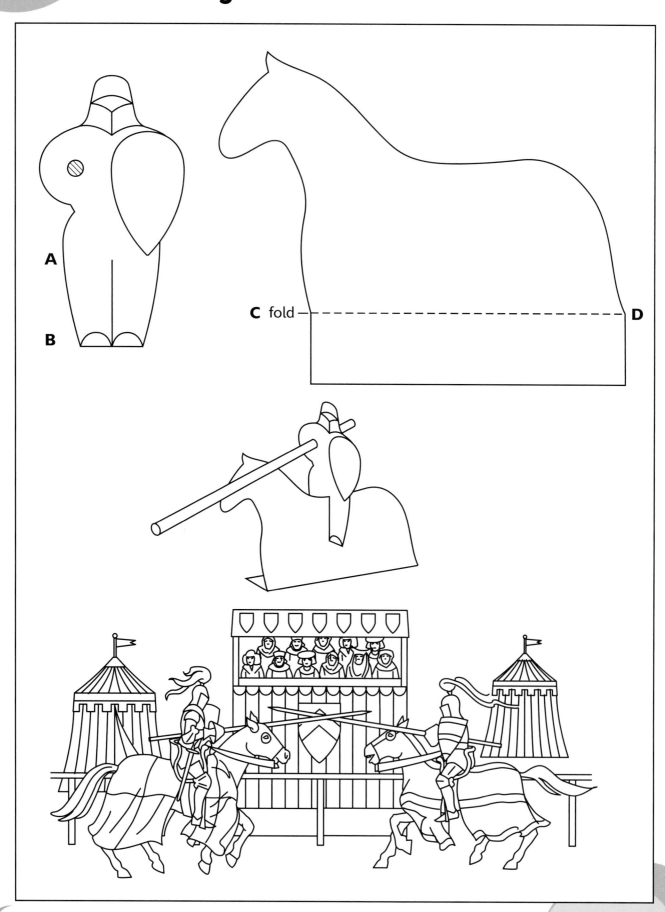

A

B

C fold

D

Theme 6 Castle dance

Music by Sally-Anne Riley

MUSIC SET BY SALLY SCOTT

Theme 6 Castle dance

1. Form two lines as in diagram 1.

2. While the music in the first two bars is being played (the beating drum), the boys bow to the girls and the girls curtsey to the boys.

3. Bar 3: On the first beat make a step forward with the left foot. On the second beat make a step forward with the right foot. On the third beat make a step forward with the left foot. On the fourth beat clap once as shown in Diagram 2.

4. Bar 4: On the first beat make a step backwards with the left foot. On the second beat make a step backwards with the right foot. On the third beat make a step backwards with the left foot. On the fourth at bend then straighten your knees.

5. Bar 5: Repeat bar 3.

6. Bar 6: Repeat bar 4 but on the fourth beat hold hands as shown in Diagram 3 and face left.

7. Bar 7: On the first beat make a step with the left foot. On the second beat make a step with the right foot. On the third beat make a step with the left foot. On the fourth beat turn and face in the opposite direction.

8. Bar 8 is a repeat of bar 7 but on the fourth beat turn and face partner again.

9. Bar 9 is a repeat of bar 3.

10. Bar 10 is a repeat of bar 4.

11. Repeat the whole of bars 3–10 but on the fourth beat of bar 10 bow or curtsey to your partner.

1.

2.

3.

Into battle

BACKGROUND

Knights in armour spring to mind when thinking about medieval battles, but archers were also important. A rain of arrows could penetrate chainmail, proving deadly to knights before they could charge the enemy. The longbow, invented in the 12th century, was about two metres long and usually made from yew. The arrows were almost a metre long and could penetrate armour at a range of 200m. A skilled archer could fire an arrow every five seconds and they had to be very fit and strong to be able to pull back the bow. Crossbows, developed in the 14th century, fired short arrows called bolts and were slower to reload than longbows. Later versions had a windlass to help wind back the bowstring, allowing soldiers with less strength than bowmen to use them.

The largest siege engine was the trebuchet (see page 63). The trebuchet has a long arm and short arm. The short arm is connected to a huge wooden box that is full of stones and acts as a counter balance. The long arm is connected to a sling. When the trebuchet is being loaded, the long arm is pulled down by ropes attached to its end and the winch. The sling is stretched out under the arms and loaded with a rock. When the ropes are released, the arm is pulled up rapidly as the counter balance comes down, and the sling whips round from underneath and opens overhead to release the stone. The mangonel was a small siege engine, used to fire drums of burning oil over the castle walls and the ballista was a catapult that fired large arrows.

If a castle could not be taken in a battle, the attacking army would hold a siege, attempting to poison the water supply, shoot in fire arrows to burn barns containing food, cause disease by hurling over dead animals, or bribe people in the castle to let them in. People in castles stored water and food in case of siege, and kept their horses and donkeys alive so that they could drink their blood to stay alive. When the food was used up, they would eat rats, mice, grass and other plants. They would also boil up the saddles and chew leather. Attempts would be made to smuggle in food and send messengers for help. If the constable held out for 40 days before surrendering he could surrender with honour.

THE CONTENTS

Lesson 1 (Ages 5–7)
Archery
The children compare a longbow and crossbow, then investigate the distances travelled by an arrow.

Lesson 2 (Ages 7–9)
The trebuchet
The children learn how a trebuchet works by making a simple model. They investigate the how far missiles can travel.

Lesson 3 (Ages 9–11)
Siege
A siege board game is played whereby the constable aims to hold out for 40 days.

Notes on photocopiables
Archery (page 62)
This sheet compares a longbow and a crossbow, with a table for recording results.

The trebuchet (page 63)
A picture of the trebuchet in action is shown, with a diagram of a simple model and a table for recording results.

Siege (page 64)
This sheet features a board game about how an attacking army try to make the people in a castle surrender.

PHOTOGRAPH © WARWICK CASTLE

Lesson 1 Archery

Objectives
● To examine how a longbow works.
● To find a relationship between the distance the bow is drawn back and the distance the arrow travels.

Subject references
Science
● Collect evidence by making measurements. (NC: KS1 Sc1 1)
● Think about what might happen before deciding what to do. (NC: KS1 Sc1 2c)
● Follow simple instructions to control the risks to themselves and others. (NC: KS1 Sc1 2e)
● Identify simple patterns. (NC: KS1 Sc1 2h)
● Understand that both pushes and pulls are examples of forces. (NC: KS1 Sc4 2b)

Resources and preparation
● Make copies of page 62, 'Archery', for every child.
● You will need toy bows and arrows with rubber sucker, a ruler, metre rule or measuring tape, pencils and a stopwatch.
● An open space such as the hall or the playground is required.
● This lesson can be adapted to be part of your Castle Day.

What to do
● Talk about the importance of the archer in battles using the information in the Background section (see page 57).
● Explain that an archer could pick up an arrow, pull it back and let it go in five seconds. Show the children the toy bows and arrows and say that you are going to time them trying to do the same.
● Now tell them that an archer could fire 12 arrows in one minute. Mime taking an arrow from a quiver mounted on the ground, inserting it in the bowstring and pulling back the bow. Ask the children to repeat the mime and time them to see how many they can fire. Some children may forget to load and pull back sufficiently in order to work fast.

● Give the children the photocopiable sheet and compare the pictures of the longbow with the crossbow. *How are they the same? How are they different?* (The longbow is held vertically and the crossbow is held horizontally; the longbow is larger, and arrows are longer than crossbow bolts; a crossbow has a winch to help pull back the bolts.)
● Ask the children what would happen if they only pulled back the string a little way on a longbow and what would happen if they pulled it back a long way. Invite them to test their ideas scientifically by carrying out an investigation.
● Depending on the age and ability of the children, you may want to perform the investigation as a demonstration and ask them to help you. Discuss safety issues before and during the investigation.
● Let the children complete the results table as they measure the amount the bow string is drawn back (A), and how far the arrow travels when fired (B).
● Discuss the importance of repeating the experiment to check the data.
● Do the results support the children's original ideas?

Extension
Draw attention to the fact that the longbow archer on the photocopiable sheet is pointing his arrow upwards. Ask the children how they could perform an investigation to see if pointing an arrow upwards makes it go further. Summarise their responses as follows: test out holding the arrow horizontally and pulling it back a certain amount, measuring the distance travelled by the arrow; repeat these steps with the arrow pointing upwards.

PHOTOGRAPH © WARWICK CASTLE

Lesson 2 The trebuchet

Resources and preparation
- Photocopy page 63, 'The trebuchet', one for each child.
- Provide a 1.5kg bag of flour.
- You will need the following for each child or group: a 15cm and a 30cm ruler, plastic straw approximately 11cm long, sticky tape, two wooden blocks (12cm × 6cm × 2cm) or equivalent, large lump of Plasticine (approximately 150g), cotton-wool balls, force meter calibrated in grams up to 150g with a small plastic bag attached to hold the lumps of Plasticine.
- This lesson can be adapted to be part of your Castle Day.

Starter
- Hold up the bag of flour and ask the children what it would be like to be hit by it. Tell them that if they were on a castle wall when a trebuchet fired they should be prepared to be hit by an object 60 times bigger (90 kg) – make its shape with your hands to demonstrate the size.

IMAGE EUBUILDIT PROJECT WARWICK UNIVERSITY HTTP://WWW.EUBUILDIT.NET © SEAN NEILL

- Hand out the photocopiable sheet and explain how the trebuchet works, using the information from the Background section (see page 57) and pointing to the different parts labelled in Figure 1. Include in your explanation that the arm is swung upwards because of the pull of gravity on the box of stones.

What to do
- Tell the children that they are going to make a simple model of the trebuchet as shown in Figure 2 on the photocopiable sheet. The model will not have a sling as the opening mechanism, because the sling is rather complicated.
- Give the children the equipment and materials they need and ask them to assemble a trebuchet using the diagram on the sheet to help them. The lump of Plasticine represents the box of stones. The small Plasticine wall represents the sling as it forces the missile forwards. In this experiment, a cotton-wool ball acts as the missile.
- As the children assemble the model, ask them to make the small retaining wall of Plasticine as thin as possible to keep the weight down.
- Instruct the children to stick the straw to the small ruler, 7cm from one end, and then onto the top of the wooden blocks.

AGES 7–9

Objectives
- To understand how a trebuchet works.
- To make a simple trebuchet.
- To use a trebuchet in a scientific investigation.

Subject references
Science
- Test ideas using evidence from observation and measurement. (NC: KS2 Sc1 1b)
- Make systematic measurements. (NC: KS2 Sc1 2f)
- Check observations and measurements by repeating them. (NC: KS2 Sc1 2g)
- Identify simple patterns. (NC: KS2 Sc1 2i)
- Objects are pulled downwards because of the gravitational attraction between them and the Earth. (NC: KS2 Sc4 2b)

ILLUSTRATION © LASZLO VERES/BEEHIVE ILLUSTRATION

● Encourage the children to experiment with their trebuchet to find a mass of Plasticine that flings the cotton-wool ball just a short way. Show them how to use the force meter to measure the mass of each lump of Plasticine. A mass of 125g will fling the missile about 36cm, so the children will need to begin with much smaller masses and work up to approximately 125g. The children can use the long ruler to measure the distances.

● Remind the children that the experiment should be repeated three times with each mass to check the measurements. During the investigation, a large lump of Plasticine may drop off but it can easily be pressed back into place.

● Encourage the children to fill in their results in the table on the photocopiable sheet.

Differentiation

● Support children by helping them to find the mass of the Plasticine and measure the distance travelled by the missile. They can fire the trebuchet just once for each mass of Plasticine.

● Ask more confident children to check through their results and look for a pattern.

Do they have any results that do not fit the pattern? If they find any, can they try and explain them?

Assessment
Assess the childrens' measuring skills with the force meter and ruler.

Plenary
Invite the children to summarise their results. They should discover that the larger the mass of the Plasticine, the greater the distance the missile is thrown. Explain that the force acting down on the short end of the trebuchet is the weight of the Plasticine, and as its mass in grams increases, its weight in newtons also increases. It is this weight – a force – which pulls down the short arm and, as the force pulling the arm down increases, the force pushing the missile into the air also increases.

Outcomes
● The children can make a simple trebuchet.

● The children can use a force meter and a ruler in an investigation.

● The children can identify a relationship from the data they collect.

HOT TOPICS Castles

Lesson 3 Seige

Resources and preparation
- Make copies of page 64, 'Siege'.
- You will need two counters, a dice and shaker per pair of children.
- Provide books featuring information about real sieges or visit:
www.castles-of-britain.com/castlest.htm
- This lesson can be adapted to be part of your Castle Day.

What to do
- Explain to the children that when an army threatened a castle, the people from the surrounding lands came into the castle for protection. The siege army had tactics to try and get the people to surrender, and the people in the castle had tactics to survive until help arrived.
- The constable, who was in charge of the castle in the lord's absence, could surrender with honour if he defied the siege army for 40 days. It would be hoped that during this time his lord would have returned with an army to rescue the castle.
- Show the children the information about sieges and ask what they think it would

have been like for those involved, including the soldiers, constable and people from the surrounding lands inside the castle.
- Hand out the photocopiable sheet and organise the children to work in pairs. Explain that one person takes the part of a soldier in the siege army and the other plays the role of the constable of the castle. The player with the highest dice roll goes first. If either player lands on their opponent's square they must move back one place. The first person to reach day 40 wins, and this decides whether the castle is taken by the siege or the constable can surrender with honour.

Extension
Invite the children to use secondary sources to find out about real sieges. They could also write about how they might feel if they were in a castle that was under siege, thinking about different viewpoints, based on the discussion earlier in the lesson.

AGES 9–11

Objectives
- To find out how attackers tried to make the people in a castle surrender when under siege.
- To find out how people in a castle tried to survive a siege.

Subject references
History
- Characteristic features of the periods and societies studied, including the experiences of men, women and children in the past. (NC: KS2 2a)
English
- Imagine and explore feelings and ideas, focusing on creative uses of language and how to interest the reader. (NC: KS2 En3 9a)

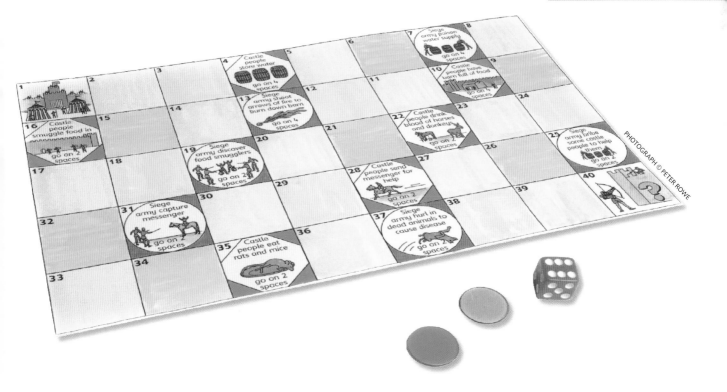

PHOTOGRAPH © PETER ROWE

SCHOLASTIC
www.scholastic.co.uk

Theme 7 Archery

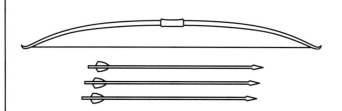

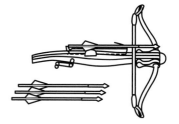

A	B
Bow string: distance drawn back (cm)	Arrow flight: distance travelled (m)

Theme 7 The trebuchet

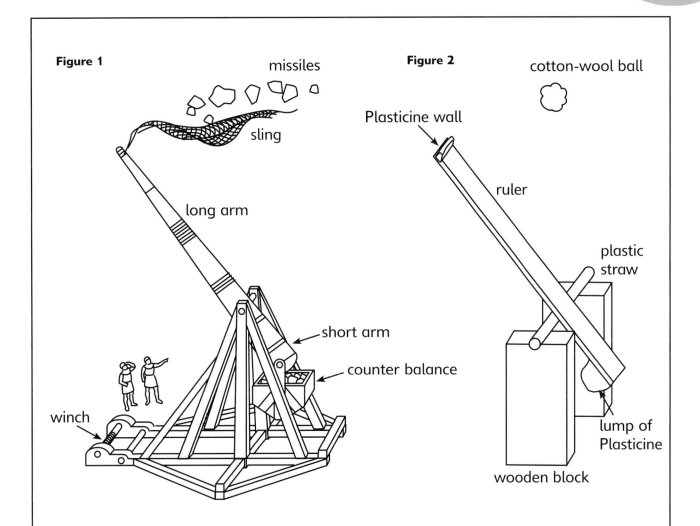

Mass of plasticine (g)	Distance travelled by cotton-wool ball (cm)		
	Attempt 1	Attempt 2	Attempt 3

Theme 7 Siege

1

2

3

4 Castle people store water. Go on 4 spaces

5

6

7 Siege army poison water supply. Go on 4 spaces

8

9

10 Castle people have barn full of food. Go on 4 spaces

11

12

13 Siege army shoot arrows of fire to burn down barn. Go on 4 spaces

14

15

16 Castle people smuggle food in. Go on 2 spaces

17

18

19 Siege army discover food smugglers. Go on 2 spaces

20

21

22 Castle people drink blood of horses and donkeys. Go on 2 spaces

23

24

25 Siege army bribe some castle people to help them. Go on 2 spaces

26

27

28 Castle people send messenger for help. Go on 2 spaces

29

30

31 Siege army capture messenger. Go on 2 spaces

32

33

34

35 Castle people eat rats and mice. Go on 2 spaces

36

37 Siege army hurl in dead animals to cause disease. Go on 2 spaces

38

39

40

The end of castles

BACKGROUND

The cannon was introduced into Europe in the early 14th century. The exploding gunpowder created a rapid expansion of gases inside the cannon that pushed out the cannon ball at great speed. Early cannons sometimes exploded, but by about 1450, they became reliable and powerful enough to destroy castle walls. Castles could not be defended against cannons and castle building stopped. In time, cannons used in the English Civil War (1642-1651) helped to destroy many remaining castles.

Before that time, however, in Tudor times, there was another reason for castle building to cease. Life became more peaceful and powerful people preferred to show off their wealth by building large houses with many glass windows.

When castle building stopped, some were abandoned, and stone and other materials were removed to make other buildings. Some castles remained as homes even when the newer grander houses became fashionable, but in the Civil War many were 'slighted' or partially destroyed after they had been captured, to prevent them being of use to the enemy. Slighting involved knocking down the walls, removing crenellations and destroying kitchens. Stone and other materials were salvaged to make new buildings.

The Civil War occurred in three stages. The first and second were between 1642–1645 and 1648–1649 respectively, between supporters of Charles I and those backing parliament. The third, in 1649–1651, was between the supporters of Charles II and parliament. During this time, many battles and skirmishes took place. Some castles involved in the conflict were Arundel, Berkely, Edinburgh, Goodrich, Nottingham, Pembroke, Sherborne, Skipton and Tenby. The Royalists wore flamboyant clothing and long hair, whereas parliamentary supporters wore more armour and had short hair, from which it is believed the term Roundhead was coined.

THE CONTENTS

IPHOTOGRAPH © PHOTODISC/GETTY IMAGES

Lesson 1 Trebuchet and cannon

Resources and preparation
● Make copies of the photcopiable pages 'The trebuchet' (page 63) and the 'Trebuchet and cannon' (page 70) for all the children.
● For each child or group to make the trebuchet (optional) provide: pencil, ruler, plastic straw approximately 11cm long, sticky tape, two wooden blocks (12cm × 6cm × 2cm) or equivalent, large lump of Plasticine, cotton wool ball.
● You will need 16 empty cardboard boxes about the size of crisp packets, a football and a whiteboard and pens.
● This lesson can be adapted to be part of your Castle Day.

What to do
● Give the children 'The trebuchet' sheet and discuss how the trebuchet works. If possible, make one as shown in the diagram and demonstrate its mechanism. Tell the children that a missile thrown by a trebuchet is similar to them making an overhead throw, like a footballer taking a throw in.
● Next, hand out the 'Trebuchet and cannon' sheet. Explain that one of the children is going to act as a human trebuchet and has to try and knock down a castle wall!
● Invite the children to make a wall out of the boxes. If they have done the exercise using mason's marks in Theme 3 Lesson 1

(page 26), remind them of it and encourage them to add their mason's marks onto the boxes.
● Ask the children what will happen when someone acts as a trebuchet and throws a football at the wall. Draw a picture on the board to match their prediction.
● Let one child throw the ball. Invite the class to record the result on the 'Trebuchet and cannon' sheet by drawing in the appropriate box.
● Rebuild the wall and explain that one of the children is going to be a 'kicking cannon'. Ask the class to predict what will happen when the ball is kicked at the wall. Draw their prediction on the board.
● Let one child kick the ball and then ask the class to record the result in the appropriate box on the sheet.
● Ask the children to compare the pictures they have drawn with the pictures of the predictions on the board. They should conclude that the cannon is more powerful than the trebuchet and knocks down more of the wall.

Extension
Repeat the experiment, but this time ask several children to take it in turns to be trebuchets and to see how many people it takes to knock down the wall completely. Other groups can take it in turns to act as cannons, to see how many turns they need to destroy the wall.

PHOTOGRAPH © PHOTODISC/GETTY IMAGES

Lesson 2 Castle ruins

Resources and preparation
● Make copies of the photocopiables 'Castle and a site plan' (page 40) and 'Castle visit' (page 71) for all the children.
● Organise a class visit to a castle, following school policies.
● Provide clipboards and pencils, and information books showing castles and their features.
● You will also need a digital camera and extra paper.

Starter
● Give the children the 'Castle and site plan' photocopiable sheet and tell them that the picture presents a typical castle. Challenge the children to identify all of the various parts. Explain that many castles have been damaged and in some places only the foundations of the buildings survive. Invite them to look at the site plan and to relate the foundations to the buildings in the pictures.
● Tell the children that they are going to visit a real castle and look for the different buildings and features it has. Hand out the 'Castle visit' photocopiable sheet and remind them about the castle features they have studied that are on the sheet.
● Additonal features included on the sheet are the sally-port, also called postern, and garderobe. The sally-port was a hidden side door that people in a castle could use to sneak out and launch a surprise attack (sally) on an attacking army or to smuggle in food and send out messengers. The garderobe was a simple toilet consisting of a seat set into the wall with a hole leading down to a moat or a cesspit. This 'seat' was curtained off for privacy.
● Use reference books to show different examples of the castle features that the children should look for, and to refresh their memories. Remember to take the sheets and extra paper with you on the visit.

What to do
● When visiting the castle, give the children clipboards, pencils and extra paper before they reach the castle. Ask them to record as much information as they can on the 'Castle visit' photocopiable sheet.
● Start by asking the children to look at the front of the castle. Encourage them to record their observations about the following features: ditch, moat, barbican (an area in front of the gatehouse which may have defensive walls) and gatehouse. Remind the children that they can make extra notes in the spaces provided.
● Take the children around the rest of the castle and point out the different features on the castle that are mentioned on the photocopiable sheet. Is there anything on the sheet that the children can no longer see on the castle? Ask them to make a note of this.
● In addition to filling in the sheet, encourage the group to make drawings of features they find interesting and to take photographs with a digital camera. (Ensure that the children only take photographs in the areas where the castle authorities permit it.)

AGES 7–9

Objectives
● To make observations of an actual castle and record them.
● To discuss findings in a group.

Subject references
History
● Find out about the events, people and changes studied from an appropriate range of sources and information. (NC: KS2 4a)
● Local history study – Investigate how a locality was affected by a significant national or local event. (NC: KS2 7)
ICT
● Develop and refine ideas by bringing together, organising and reorganising texts and images. (NC: KS2 2a)

PHOTOGRAPH © VINCE ED. STOCK.XCHNG

PHOTOGRAPH © 2007, NEELA MANN WWW.SUDELEYCASTLE.CO.UK

Differentiation

- Some children may need help in identifying some of the smaller features, such as arrow loops or the numbers of floors and fireplaces.
- More confident learners should be encouraged to make notes wherever possible including details such as which way the staircases spiral upwards. Staircases that spiral upwards in a clockwise direction are easier to defend from above, as the right hand of the defending soldier can be used to swing a sword down, but the right hand of the attacking soldier is blocked from swinging a sword upwards. (Refer to the Background section of Theme 3 on page 25 for detail of this kind.)

Assessment

Compare the items ticked by the children with the items that were actually present in the castle. The quality of the notes and any additional drawings and images can also be assessed.

Did you know?

A cesspit beneath a garderobe was galled a gong. It was emptied by a gong farmer.

Plenary

Back in the classroom, ask the children to discuss their findings and make reports using a range of ICT packages. They could work towards a classroom display or even a website based on the castle that they visited. Alternatively they could prepare presentations to give to other children in the school, and this could be done on your school's Castle Day.

Outcomes

- The children can make observations on a castle and record them.
- The children can produce a report of their visit.

Lesson 3 Castles in the Civil War

Resources and preparation
- Photocopy page 72, 'When was the Civil War?', one for each child.
- You will need scissors, sheet of white A4 paper, and rulers.
- Provid secondary sources about Romans, Vikings, Anglo-Saxons, Normans, Tudors, Victorians and the Second World War or visit **http://easyweb.easynet.co.uk/~crossby/ECW/index.htm** which provides a large amount of information written at an appropriate level for children about the Civil War. Many other periods of history are covered at **www.bbc.co.uk/schools/websites/4_11/site/history.shtml** and for information on the Normans visit **http://www.historyforkids.org/learn/medieval/history/highmiddle/normans.htm**

What to do
- Hand out the photocopiable sheet 'When was the Civil War?' and invite the children to cut out the time periods and arrange them into chronological order. (Revise the term chronological if necessary.)
- Invite the children to make a timeline. They can do this by folding a piece of A4 paper in half (from landscape), using the fold as the basis of their timeline. Instruct the children to mark a point about 4cm in from the left, to act as zero. Then ask them to draw a line along the fold from the zero point, measuring 21cm across. They then need to divide the line into 1cm sections, whereby 1cm is equal to 100 years.
- Ask the children to use a ruler to mark out the decades that relate to the beginnings and ends of each time period they have cut out, starting with the Romans. They can then connect the lines between the beginning and ends of each period, and add a label for each era. Suggest placing some periods above and some periods below the line, and at different distances from the line, so that the periods and labels are as clear and spaced out as possible.
- Alternatively a much larger timeline can be produced to go on a wall in the classroom and groups of children can contribute information about each period.

Extension
Ask the children to compare the clothing of the Cavalier and the Roundhead on the photocopiable sheet so that they can recognise a Royalist or Parliamentarian by what they would have worn. They can compare the outfits of both men with the suit of armour on page 47 and the clothes of the castle people on page 38.

AGES 9–11

Objectives
- To place the period of castle building and the Civil War in a timeline with other periods that the children have studied.
- To appreciate that the people who took part in the Civil War dressed differently from castle people of earlier ages.

Subject references
History
- Place events, people and changes into correct periods of time.
(NC: KS2 1a)
- Use dates and vocabulary relating to the passing of time.
(NC: KS2 1b)

ILLUSTRATION © LASZLO VERES/BEEHIVE ILLUSTRATION

HOT TOPICS Castles

Theme 8 Trebuchet and cannon

wall of boxes

What does the wall of boxes look like now?

trebuchet

What does the wall of boxes look like now?

cannon

HOT TOPICS Castles

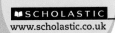

Theme 8 Castle visit

Castle	Date of visit	Name

Ditch/moat ☐
Barbican ☐

Gatehouse ☐
crenellations ☐
drawbridge ☐
portcullis ☐
murder holes ☐
doors ☐
arrow loops ☐
crest on archway ☐

Walls ☐
crenellations ☐
arrow loops ☐
sally-port/postern ☐
walkway ☐

Towers ☐
crenellations ☐
square ☐
round ☐
arrow loops ☐
spiral staircase ☐

Keep ☐
crenellations ☐
number of floors ☐
number of fire places ☐
arrow loops ☐
inside stairs ☐
garderobe ☐
dungeon ☐

Other buildings ☐
Great Hall ☐
solar chapel ☐
chapel ☐
kitchen ☐
cell ☐
barn ☐
armoury ☐
stables ☐

Theme 8 When was the Civil War?

Roundhead pikeman
(Parliamentarian)

Cavalier cavalryman
(Royalist)

Cut out the following time periods, arrange them into chronological order and set them out on a timeline.

Second World War 1939–1945	Romans in Britain AD43–410	Victorians 1837–1901	Anglo Saxons AD449 –1066
Civil War 1642–1651	Normans 1066–1154	Vikings AD793–1066	Tudors 1485—1603

Stories and legends

BACKGROUND

Castles inspire people to make up a wide range of stories and legends. Traditional children's stories such as 'Rapunzel' feature castles, while the castle of Camelot is home to the legendary King Arthur and his Knights of the Round Table. Many castles have their stories of ghosts. A survey in one primary school asked children, *What do you think about when you think about castles?* Year 3 children said *Scary places*, while Year 5 enjoyed gory stories and Year 6 children preferred to reflect on what it was like to live in a castle.

In this theme, we look at how a castle can feature in a story (Lesson 1) and how it has inspired tales of hauntings (Lesson 2). There is no intention to become involved with considerations of the supernatural, but simply to reflect the tradition that castles inspire ghost stories and many people enjoy them. The lessons should be approached in a light-hearted way, and this is reflected in the last sentence of 'The haunted castle' story when the actual reader becomes a ghost. The story used here has been inspired by actual stories in castles and the author has combined these aspects with invention, so that many things occur in just one castle. In Lesson 3, the children focus on what they have learned about castles and produce an account about castle life.

THE CONTENTS

Lesson 1 (Ages 5–7)
Bodwin's bouncy castle
The children listen to a story about a witch and a bouncy castle, and answer questions about it.

Lesson 2 (Ages 7–9)
The haunted castle
The children listen to a story of a visit to a haunted castle, then read it for themselves and identify the ghosts.

Lesson 3 (Ages 9–11)
The story of a castle
The children use the information they have gathered in this topic to tell the story of a castle or castle life.

Notes on photocopiables
Bodwin's bouncy castle (page 78)
This simple story features names used in medieval times. The children answer questions on the story, and older children can read it and develop it into a simple play.

The haunted castle (page 79)
The answers to the questions are:
The person reading the story has become a ghost; Q1) The ghost in the moat was the bear; Q2) The ghost of the falcon and horses' hooves is related to the lord killed while out hunting; Q3) The ghost of the executed lady is the faceless head; Q4) The ghosts in the dungeon are of the six prisoners starved to death; Q5) The ghost of the person drowned in the well is the person in the wet red dress; Q6) The ghost on the drawbridge is the ghost of the messenger; Q7) The ghosts by the wall are of the soldiers pelted with stones; Q8) The ghost of the dog is the ghost of the animal with the stab wounds (the portcullis dropped on it); Q9) The sound of breaking glass is related to the lord killed by poisoned wine; Q10) The ghost in the armour was the lord maimed in battle.

There is no photocopiable for Lesson 3.

PHOTOGRAPH © PHOTODISC/GETTY IMAGES

LESSON 1 Bodwin's bouncy castle

AGES 5–7

Objectives
● To test the children's listening skills by telling them a story and asking questions about it.

Subject references
English
● Sustain concentration. (NC: KS1 En1 2a)
● Remember specific point that interest them. (NC: KS1 En1 2b)
● Make relevant comments. (NC: KS1 En1 2c)
● Listen to others' reactions. (NC: KS1 En1 2d)
● Take turns in speaking. (NC: KS1 En1 3a)
● Relate their contributions to what has gone on before. (NC: KS1 En1 3b)
● Extend their ideas in the light of discussion. (NC: KS1 En1 3d)

Resources and preparation
● Photocopy page 78, 'Bodwin's Bouncy Castle', one for each child.
● Provide books containing stories that feature castles.
● This lesson can be adapted to be part of your Castle Day.

What to do
● Explain to the children that some people travel around telling stories. Invite them to imagine that they are the children in a castle and you are a visiting storyteller. Let them gather at your feet and read the story on the photocopiable sheet.
● When you have finished, ask the children about points in the story, discussing why they think certain things happened, and the different characters.

● Encourage the children to think about how the story might continue. For example, say that you think that as the witch bounced past the king, he decided to find out where she came from. When the king arrived at the bouncy castle and learned of Bodwin's spell he made Bodwin a knight! The wizard lived on in the castle for the rest of his days.
● Alternatively, older children could read the story themselves and discuss it in small groups.
● Show the class the information books featuring stories about castles and read them to the children. Which stories do they like the best? Do they prefer the first story they heard? What parts of the different stories do they enjoy the most?

Extension
The story on the photocopiable sheet can be developed into a simple play in which the children enjoy being the people jumping around in the bouncy castle. Alternatively, read other stories to the children that feature castles and ask them questions to test their listening skills.

LESSON 2 The haunted castle

Resources and preparation
● Make copies of 'The haunted castle' photocopiable sheet (page 79).
● This lesson can be adapted to be part of your Castle Day.

Starter
Ask the children what they think is scary about a castle. Some might say that it is the dark passages, the spiral staircases or the dungeons. It is likely that in this conversation the topic of ghosts will arise and you can use this opening to introduce the story on the photocopiable sheet.

What to do
● Say to the children that you are going to read an account of visiting a castle and explain that the events they will hear about are based on stories that are told in many castles in the British Isles. Emphasise that these tales are only stories. Ask the children to listen carefully to the story, as they will have to try and identify the ghosts at the end.
● Gather the children round and tell them the story. (Be sensitive to some of the children who may be easily scared and keep the story light-hearted.)

● At the end of the story, ask the children if they can identify each of the ghosts. Do not keep a record of the answers and at the end of the discussion let the children go back to their tables and then give out copies of the photocopiable sheet.
● Encourage the children to read through the story again on their own or in pairs. Then, ask them to answer the questions at the bottom of sheet and identify the ghosts.
● When they have finished, discuss the children's answers. Were they able to identify all of the ghosts?
● The children can now use their own imaginations and inspiration from the photocopiable story to write their own scary castle tales.
● The creative writing activity is also a great opportunity for drama and oral storytelling. Ask the children to read aloud their story to a partner, and choose some pairs to retell their partner's story to the rest of the class. Select some of the best stories produced and organise the children into small groups to devise short performances of their allocated story.

PHOTOGRAPH © SEAN JOHNSON, STOCK.XCHNG

Did you know?
Castles with pointed roofed towers sometimes seen in fairy tale books were built in Europe.

Differentiation
- Some children will need help in linking the story with the ghosts.
- Ask more confident learners to rank the ghosts in order of scariness on a league table!
- For the creative writing activity assist less confident learners by providing them with starter sentences and written prompts to help them devise a story with a beginning, middle and end.
- Organise the children into mixed-ability groups for the drama activity so that less confident learners are supported by their more confident peers.

Assessment
The children can be assessed by how well they identify the ghosts.

Plenary
Go through the answers with the children and if 'scariness league tables' have been produced, write them on the board and discuss them with the class.

Outcomes
- The children can listen carefully and answer questions on what they have heard.
- The children can extract information